D0467144

MANAGING STRESS
Keeping Calm under Fire

Barbara J. Braham

Professional Publishing
Burr Ridge, Illinois
New York, New York

For Rick, who has taught me the inner balance called peace,
and the outer balance called joy.

Being in Movement is a registered trademark of Paul Linden

© RICHARD D. IRWIN, INC., 1994

Sponsoring editor: Cynthia A. Zigmund
Project editor: Karen J. Nelson
Assistant production manager: Jon Christopher
Art manager: Kim Meriwether
Compositor: Wm. C. Brown Communications
Typeface: 11/13 Palatino
Printer: Book Press

Library of Congress Cataloging-in-Publication Data

Braham, Barbara J.
    Managing stress: keeping calm under fire / Barbara J. Braham.
        p.   cm.—(Briefcase books series)
    ISBN 1–55623–855–X   0–7863–0204–6 (Paperback)
    1. Stress management.   I. Title.   II. Series.
    RA785.B73   1994
    155.9′042—dc20   93–8155

Printed in the United States of America

1 2 3 4 5 6 7 8 9 0 BP 0 9 8 7 6 5 4 3

The *Briefcase Books* Series

Research shows that people who buy business books (1) want books that can be read quickly, perhaps on a plane trip, commuting on a train, or overnight, and (2) feel their time and money were well spent if they get two or three useful insights or techniques for improving their professional skills or helping them with a current problem at work.

Briefcase Books were designed to meet these two criteria. They focus on necessary skills and problem areas, and include real-world examples from practicing managers and professionals. Inside these books you'll find useful, practical information and techniques in a straightforward, concise, and easy-to-read format.

This book and others like it in the Briefcase Books series can quickly give you insights and answers regarding your current needs and problems. And they are useful references for future situations and problems.

If you find this book or any other in this series to be of value, please share it with your coworkers. With tens of thousands of new books published each year, any book that can simplify the growing complexities in managing others needs to be circulated as widely as possible.

Robert B. Nelson
Series Editor

The *Briefcase Books* Series

Managing Stress: Keeping Calm under Fire
Barbara J. Braham

Business Negotiating Basics
Peter Economy

Straight Answers to People Problems
Fred E. Jandt

Empowering Employees through Delegation
Robert B. Nelson

The Presentation Primer: Getting Your Point Across
Robert B. Nelson
Jennifer Wallick

What Did You Say? A Guide to Effective Listening
Arthur Robertson

Foreword for the Briefcase Books Series

My mission in life has been to be a conveyor of simple truths. It is for that reason that I'm pleased to be able to introduce the Briefcase Books series, which seeks to provide simple, practical, and direct answers to the most common problems managers face on a daily basis.

It has been my experience that in the field of business common sense is not common practice. So it is refreshing to find a series of books that glorifies common sense in dealing with people in the workplace.

Take the skill of listening. We all know that it is important to listen, yet how many of us actually do it well? I suggest it would be rare to find one in a hundred managers that is truly a good listener. Most people focus on what they are going to say next when someone else is talking. They would seldom if ever think to check what they thought they heard to make sure it is accurate. And they seldom acknowledge or attempt to deal with emotions when they occur in speaking with someone at work. These are basic errors in the use of this basic skill. And regardless of how much education or experience you have, you should know how to listen.

But how much training have you had on the topic of listening? Have you ever had a course on the topic? Have you ever tested your ability to listen? Have you ever discussed with others how you could listen better with greater comprehension and respect? Probably not. Even though this fundamental interpersonal skill could cripple the most talented individual if he or she is not good at it.

Fortunately, listening is just one of the fundamental skills singled out for its own volume in the Briefcase Books series. Others include books on making presentations, negotiating, problem solving, and handling stress. And other volumes are planned even as I write this.

The Briefcase Books series focuses on those basic skills that managers must master to excel at work. Whether you are new to managing or are a seasoned manager, you'll find these books of value in obtaining useful insights and fundamental knowledge you can use for your entire career.

Ken Blanchard
Co-author
The One Minute Manager

Preface

If you picked up this book, there's a good chance you or someone you care about is under stress. You want a way to manage stress that won't create more stress. What you *don't* need is a long list of techniques that you can't apply or won't apply that make you feel guilty and more stressed. What you *do* need is a philosophy that will guide you out of your stressed-out world into a place of calm and peace. You need an approach to the problem of stress that will work for you at work, at home, and with friends. You need a friendly guide that is easy to understand and helps you choose the behaviors that will reduce your stress.

This book is that guide. It tells you step by step how to be calm. It doesn't preach or judge. There are no *shoulds*. What it does is present a simple philosophy for living your life that will lead to balance and peace of mind. It doesn't tell you what to do; instead it empowers you to decide what to do. You'll learn how to take charge of your life without struggle, resistance, or trying harder.

The cornerstone of the approach is to be CALM. CALM is an acronym that stands for change the situation, accept what can't be changed, let go, and manage your lifestyle. Thus the book is about both treatment and prevention. You'll learn what to do when you're feeling stressed (the first three steps), and how to increase your capacity to respond to life's demands so that you feel stressed less often (the last step).

Three themes run throughout the book. First, to manage your stress requires that you be willing to experience short-term pain for long-term gain. This runs counter to American culture, which emphasizes short-term gain over long-term pain. To insure long-term comfort, health, and well-being may require short-term discomfort. A classic example is exercise. When you begin an exercise program, it's hard—hard to make the time, hard to run the block, or complete the workout. You'll be tempted to give up and quit. That's why you need a philosophy, a set of beliefs that will motivate you to make wise choices, not easy choices. When someone asks you to serve on a committee, it's easy to say yes. That makes them happy and you feel good—in the short term, but how do you feel when you're attending committee meetings instead of being with your family or working on your priority projects? Then do you wish you'd chosen the short-term pain of saying no for the long-term gain of less stress? A bias in this book is that stress management isn't a technique to feel better fast; rather it's a strategic decision to daily invest in your future health and well-being.

Second, the philosophy expressed is filled with paradox. Managing stress is not a matter of either/or. It's about *and*. For example, less is more. When you learn to do less, expect less of yourself (for you perfectionists), you discover you have more energy, more time for yourself, and more to give to others.

Soft is hard. Holding your body rigid when you're under stress makes you vulnerable. You can break. It's only when you learn to let your muscles go, let the breath go, and become soft that you connect with your inner sense of power so that you're empowered to take action.

To gain control, relinquish it. When you are controlling, it leads to rigidity. You lose your flexibility and your ability to respond to situations. As soon as you let go of the control and allow life to happen, you have more ability to respond instead of react. Your responsiveness gives you control your reactiveness can never achieve.

You are perfect in your imperfection. Perfectionism leads to stress. When you learn to accept your imperfection, life becomes a journey of discovery instead of an event to be judged. As you master these and other paradoxes, you'll be well on your way to staying calm.

Third, when you learn to manage stress, you enter a different way of *being*. Instead of being frantic, frazzled, and burned out, you'll learn to be calm, centered, and peaceful. The CALM model will help you stop worrying about the past or the future and live in the present. You and stress don't have to be adversaries. You can learn to blend and flow. You don't have to fight or flee when you're under stress. Stress can be your ally. You can be calm and productive.

No matter how discouraged and stressed out you may be feeling right now, there is hope. Once you learn the four easy steps to be calm, you have a companion for life. This isn't a book that is going to go out of date like a piece of computer equipment. You're investing in something that will shape the quality of your life for years to come. Don't wait any longer to calm down. Everything you need is in these pages. Turn to Chapter One and let's get started.

Acknowledgments

Thanks to Rick Sullivan for the serene seaside writing retreat where I could practice being calm; Jane and Granville Braham for their love and support; Judy Latshaw for typing the manuscript; Connie Evener for testing many of the ideas; Esther Nebiker for teaching me what it means to be calm through her presence; Mary Struble for teaching me how to meditate; Paul Linden, my Aikido instructor, for showing me through my body that soft is hard; Bill Bickham for breakfast conversations that always brought clarity; Robert Nelson for his valuable editorial suggestions; and the thousands of people who have taken my stress-management workshops and shared their lives with me.

Barbara J. Braham

Contents

Chapter Five
The M of CALM: MANAGE YOUR LIFESTYLE   146

Chapter One

Assess Your Stress

"Calm down," he said. "If you don't, you may not come out of the next one alive."

Sure, that's easy for him to say, Allan thought, as he lay in bed recovering from a sudden heart attack. He'd been trying to do that for months, but it wasn't working. How can you expect a guy to calm down when he has to deal with irate customers, constant deadlines, an impossible boss, and demands to do more, more, more?

No matter what kind of stress you face in your life, there are ways you can calm down. This book will show you how.

WHAT CAUSES STRESS?

Stress can be caused by just about anything: deadlines, traffic, public speaking, the boss, meetings, organizational change, and so on. Ask any number of people what causes them stress and each will give you a different list because everyone perceives stress differently. The causes of stress can be grouped into four major categories: change, sneaking stress, personal traits, and environmental stressors.

Change

It used to be that you could think of your life as a gradually ascending line. The American dream promised that for each generation the starting point would be a little higher than it was the generation before, and the ending point would also be higher. But what used to be true is true no more.

Today, it isn't accurate to think of your life as an upward ascending line, or even a line at all. A better analogy is a spiral. While your life will certainly have periods of upward growth, it will also most assuredly have times when you feel as if you are moving backwards. Those times when the spiral moves backwards or down are usually associated with change.

In the past, change was infrequent. Today it is rapid. You can expect a major change in your life every three to four years. Your grandparents expected three to four major changes in their lifetime! You will likely have three or more careers. You will probably work for a company that goes through substantial organizational change. Throughout your life, you will be asked to adapt to a variety of changing technologies. It is unlikely that you will spend your adult years in the traditional nuclear family— father employed and mother at home with children. More likely you will be part of a blended or single-parent family at some time in your adult life. If you are in a two-parent family, both adults will likely work outside the home. Running that home has become more complex, rather than simpler, as technology has exploded and choices have mushroomed.[1]

In the 1990s, change is the norm, and stability is the unexpected visitor. If you haven't adjusted your thinking to this truth, you will add stress to the already stressful changes in your life. You need to become a change master, not a change victim. You need to learn how to flow through times of transition and change, not fight and resist them, or flee from them. Fight and flight are two well-known stress responses that won't serve you well in the 1990s. Ironically, these strategies only make things worse.

How do you learn to flow instead? First, by understanding the change process. There are normal, predictable stages that you go through during a change. When you can identify these for yourself, you can manage yourself through them. It's a little like watching the seasons change. You've learned that the seasons are predictable and that there are things you can do to prepare for each one. If you want tulips in the spring, you plant bulbs in the fall. You plant in the spring for vegetables in the summer. And so it is with change. As you learn to master the stages, you'll discover that actions you take in one stage will lay the foundation for how well you accept the change in later stages.

There are four stages you go through during a change.[2] The first is denial. During this stage you find it hard to believe that the way you've been doing things won't continue to work. You may deny that a change needs to be made, or, if a change has been announced, or is on the way, you may find yourself denying that it will really happen. If it is a change that you don't want, your denial will likely last longer. If the change is a happy occasion, you may express denial in the form of "I can't believe it's true! I can't believe my good fortune." Whether short- or long-lived, denial is a stage we all move through. It isn't a problem unless you get stuck there.

Once you break through your denial and realize that a change *is* going to occur, the next thing that happens is that you begin to resist the change. You may resist giving up the old ways, or you may resist what is new. This is the classic "fight or flight" response. Along with resistance usually come emotions—anger, guilt, frustration, sadness, confusion, and fear, to name a few. Many people are not emotionally literate. When they experience these feelings, they don't know how to handle them, and stress often results. During resistance you struggle to find a way to integrate what is new into your previous way of being and doing. Think of it as being like bringing home a new piece of furniture. You need to find a way to fit the new chair into your living room. Perhaps there's a spot ready and waiting (those are changes you want in your life), or you may need to rearrange the room to make a space. Perhaps you'll need to discard a table or another chair to make room for the new one. Resistance is that period of time when you're moving furniture, deciding what to keep and what to let go, to accommodate your new chair. The length of time it takes in this stage varies from person to person and situation to situation. Sometimes you can rearrange your living room on the first try and it works. Other times it takes many efforts before you find a layout that you're comfortable with.

After you've integrated the change, you can set about the next stage, which is exploring the new opportunities that the change has made possible. The fight or flight response of the resistance phase has ended; now you can flow. During this exploratory period you look for ways you can maximize the benefits of the change. It's the time to look for rainbows. During the denial and resistance phases, you were focused on the disadvantages of the change; now you focus on what is potentially good. You look for ways to leverage the change in your behalf. In this stage you balance the polarity. Change isn't good or bad; it's both. Charles Dickens captured it well in the opening lines of his novel, *A Tale of Two Cities:*

> It was the best of times, it was the worst of times;
> It was the age of wisdom, it was the age of foolishness;
> It was the epoch of belief, it was the epoch of incredulity;
> It was the season of light, it was the season of darkness;
> It was the spring of hope, it was the winter of despair.[3]

As you move through the third stage, you reach the final stage of acceptance. You can now see clearly what is positive *and* negative about the change. You have integrated the change into your life and you're ready to go on, to move on in your life. This particular change ceases to consume major amounts of your time or energy. It has become woven into the tapestry of your life.

At any stage you can get stuck and not move forward. When that happens, your whole life feels stuck. It's like being stuck in a snowdrift. You can rev your engine, burn up lots of gas, spin your tires, and burn rubber. Still, you go nowhere. When you do this emotionally, you burn yourself out. Being a change master means you can recognize a snowdrift. You know how to avoid them, or get out of them if you do get stuck. In today's world the snow isn't going to go away. Paradoxically, the only way out is through, and, when you get through this drift, there will be another one around the corner waiting. Thus you may have relative stability in your personal life, but your company is going through a merger. Perhaps your work world is stable, but you have an aging parent that needs your care. You can be sure that "there's always something." Get used to it! Accept this new truth of living in the 1990s. Your ability to transform difficulties and problems into challenges is a key to your becoming a change master and a stress manager.

Changes fall into two major categories: the ones you want, and therefore tend to view as positive, and those you don't want or didn't expect, which you view more negatively.

Desired changes. These changes you anticipate with excitement; you look forward to them. For example, a new project, a move to a new location, retirement, marriage, and promotion are all things you might perceive as positive. Although that doesn't make them less stressful, it does change your *attitude* about the stress. As you plan for these changes, you will probably feel invigorated and excited. In fact, you usually choose these stressors in your life! Because you choose them and generally view them as positive and exciting, desired changes are rarely the reason you seek "stress management" information.

Gordon Brim in his book *Ambition* points out that even reaching your goals can be stressful. ". . . we rarely change behavior after winning. Instead we shorten our timetables and speed up our plans for achievement. We raise our aspirations. We add new goals. In some ways winning is harder to manage than losing."[4]

Unexpected changes. Unlike desired changes, unanticipated changes are usually negative and sometimes devastating. A disabling accident, death, illness, reorganization, layoff, a new boss, a lost customer, new government regulations, and marketplace changes are all examples of unexpected, unplanned changes. Such situations create acute, short-term stress, and sometimes long-term stress. Because of their dramatic nature, you usually turn to colleagues, friends, and family for support. Therefore, despite their intensity, the changes do not usually create long-term stress-management problems.

Exceptions to this occur if you're required to keep the change a secret, or if you have no emotional support. For example, knowledge of a pending downsizing or reorganization that you cannot discuss creates more stress than if you could talk openly about it. Being laid off with no support networks is more stressful than if you have lots of emotional and financial supports.

Not all unexpected changes are negative, however. You might win the lottery! Yet research on lottery winners shows that many of those who have this unexpected good fortune have difficulty handling the stress that comes with it. Despite their massive wins, they end up bankrupt. There are numerous examples of people who experienced great success early in life and never recovered. In fact, history is filled with examples of famous performers who, after achieving stardom in their teens or early twenties, were unable to manage the stress of their success and committed suicide. Surprising as it might seem, winning big is as difficult to manage as losing big.

"Sneaking" Stress

This is a significant cause of distress for most people. "Sneaking" stressors are the little things that add up, the "straw that breaks the camel's back." Consider the morning you oversleep, burn the toast, discover you're out of coffee, and hit every red light on the way to the office! Does this sound familiar? After a couple of these days you discover you are feeling stressed. The stress doesn't result from any one major event, as with desired or unexpected changes. Rather, it results from a series of small stressors that sneak up on you until one morning you awaken with some symptom.

Also included in sneaking stress are the "isms." Sexism, racism, ageism, classism, and so forth. Any condition that continuously drains off a percentage of your energy is a sneaking stressor. If you have financial pressures, you may not have a bill collector calling you today, but you have the ever-present concern of how you will make ends meet.

If you have a handicapping condition or serious illness, or care for someone who does, that too can become a sneaking stressor because it is always there draining off part of your available energy for managing life's stress. If you live an alternative lifestyle, or are a victim of sexual harassment, those too are examples of sneaking stress.

For many people, particularly those in midlife (defined as 35 to 65), it is a lack of purpose that is a sneaking stressor. Do you love what you're doing, or has your work started to lose its meaning? After the greed of the '80s, many people today want to simplify their lives and live their values instead of living an image. They want to make more than a living; they want to make a life.

If you want more meaningful work, here are some concrete steps you can take. First, do you need to revitalize what you're doing now? Perhaps you are working on purpose, but you've lost touch with it. Dennis Jaffee and Cynthia Scott in their best-selling book *Take This Job and Love It* write, "Many times it is not the nature of the job itself, but the inner baggage of negative and limiting beliefs and expectations, that turns off the energy and excitement you could have at work."[5] Ask yourself these questions to determine if you need to revitalize your current job.

1. Look at your expectations. Are they realistic?

2. Look at your attitude. Are you confusing mistakes with failures? Mistakes are learning opportunities; failures kill self-esteem.

3. Where are you in your life cycle? In the first 10 to 20 years of your career, your focus is appropriately on skill development and establishing your competency. After you have acquired a set of skills, your focus moves inward. How can you use those skills to make a difference and be of service to others? A concern with meaning and purpose is therefore largely a developmental issue. Moving through this transition doesn't necessarily mean you need to change careers. It may mean you need to decide how to make a difference with your competencies.

4. Are you a risk taker? If you always play it safe in search of stability and security, you may or may not find it. One thing is for sure: you run the risk of feeling bored with what you're doing. Boredom is as much a cause of burnout as overload. Be willing to stretch yourself and keep learning; keep looking for new ways to do your

current tasks. You can be creative in how you approach your work.

5. Enrich yourself and your work. Do you take responsibility for your own learning? In today's world you need to become a lifelong learner to stay marketable. Don't expect your boss to be responsible for your professional growth. Create your own challenges.

Mihaly Csikszentmihalyi, professor of psychology at the University of Chicago and author of *Flow: The Psychology of Optimum Experience,* studied people from a wide variety of industries, ranging from farmers to factory workers. In every field he was able to find people who found their work to be meaningful and interesting because of their approach to it. Doing a repetitive function on a factory assembly line is not an inherently meaningful type of work. However, it can be made meaningful if you choose to. Here's what Csikszentmihalyi discovered in his research.

Those people who enjoyed their work and reached a state of flow had in common these eight characteristics:

First, the experience usually occurs when we confront tasks we have a chance of completing. Second, we must be able to concentrate on what we are doing. Third and fourth, the concentration is usually possible because the task undertaken has clear goals and provides immediate feedback. Fifth, one acts with a deep but effortless involvement that removes from awareness the worries and frustrations of everyday life. Sixth, enjoyable experiences allow people to exercise a sense of control over their actions. Seventh, concern for the self disappears, yet paradoxically the sense of self emerges stronger after the flow experience is over. Finally, the sense of the duration of time is altered; hours pass by in minutes, and minutes can stretch out to seem like hours.[6]

Thus, if you choose to take control of your situation, you can turn it into a meaningful experience.

If these suggestions from Jaffe, Scott, and Csikszent-mihalyi on how to revitalize your work haven't answered your questions, then perhaps you need a change of work or career. How do you determine what that new career might be? Through an introspective process designed to help you discover your purpose.

The process starts within you, not externally with the job market or your skills. Starting from the outside and working in—as most people do—can cause stress because you meet other people's needs instead of your own. Working from the inside out requires more courage and a willingness to risk. It is also the path that will connect you with your purpose and give you a life of integrity.

To find work that you will enjoy, the first questions you need to ask yourself are "What do I *want* to do? What excites me? What do I feel passionate about?" These questions can help you identify an intangible, internal magnet that will draw you toward yourself. Others have referred to this as a calling, a vocation, the music within, or following your bliss. We'll use the word *passion* here because it literally says it all. Look at the word carefully and you see Pass-I-On. That's what meaningful work is all about. It is your ability to give yourself away through your contributions and service to others. Everyone has a unique contribution to make. When you are aligned with that purpose, you experience less stress than when you aren't.

Take some time right now to think about *your* passion. At this point you do not want to censor anything. Give all of your thoughts equal consideration. There is plenty of time to play critic later. Don't be surprised if you come up with a big question mark. What *is* my passion? To know your passion requires that you have some time to stop and reflect. We get so busy at times that we forget to stop and take any personal time alone to think about what we want. If you begin to take time each day for relaxation or meditation as recommended in Chapter 5, you will find that answers to this question begin to bubble up and make themselves known to you.

Another reason that you may have trouble answering this question is that you spend too much time worrying about what other people will think. Consequently, no sooner does a thought present itself than you begin to look at it through your spouse's eyes, your parent's eyes, your friends' eyes, and so on. If you anticipate rejection or a challenge from any of these people, you discount the thought almost before it emerges.

There are two fears that may hide your passion from you. First, your passion may be hidden because your energies are poured into avoiding what you don't want rather than striving for what you do want. Take Murray for example. He has spent the past 20 years trying to avoid poverty. He has built a successful business in the process, but he feels driven in his work. No matter how well he is doing, he fears that the next quarter his luck may turn. Therefore, he feels an imminent sense of gloom and worries all the time. He suffers from ulcers and despite his external successes doesn't feel happy with his work or lifestyle. If Murray were following his passion, he would create his business around what he wants, not what he hopes to avoid.

Second, you may know what you want to do, but you are afraid of the risks. You lack the courage to take action on your passion. When you make a commitment to yourself to follow your passion, then you begin to carefully study how you can convert your dream into a reality. This might be better called *calculated risk taking*. From this perspective it does not feel risky. As Goethe said, "The moment one definitely commits oneself, then providence moves too. All sorts of things occur to help one that would never otherwise have occurred. A whole stream of events issues from the decision, raising in one's favor all manner of unforeseen incidents and meetings and material assistance which no man could have dreamed would have come his way."[7] Don't let fear keep you from seeing what it is you really want to do.

You may fail to explore your passion because you think you aren't good enough or smart enough or educated enough or _____ enough. You can fill in the blank however you want. The point is, your self-esteem is slipping. You'll learn in Chapter 4 that low self-esteem is the source of many traits that create stress for you. Not liking or believing in yourself can prevent you from being willing to go after what you want. The truth is, if you feel a passion inside yourself, you can begin to bring it into reality right now. That is not to say you won't need to start with small steps, but you don't need to have everything perfect before you start. You are okay right now the way you are.

Finally, your passion can hide behind the dollar sign. Of course you need an income to be able to manage in this society. Too often, though, the dollar sign becomes the reason for doing or not doing something. We fail to realize that money is the reward that comes from our unique service to others. Money is not the goal. This confusion has resulted in an ever more competitive culture where success is measured in dollars and cents. Jennifer James in *Success Is the Quality of Your Journey* says it well: "Remember, when you can, that the definition of success has changed. It is not only survival, the having—it is the quality of every moment of your life, the being. Success is not a destination, a place you can ever get to; it is the quality of the journey."[8]

You begin the process of finding more satisfying work by looking inside and seeing what you feel drawn to do. Once this step has been completed, and it may take some time, you can move forward with more conventional career planning.

Then you can look at the kinds of work that would allow you to fulfill your passion. You can consider what companies will provide you with the best environment for using your skills, and you can begin to think about the kinds of people you want to work with. Don't be limited by your past experience or your education. Because you were trained as a lawyer doesn't mean you will enjoy practicing law. Take Dennis for example.

Dennis had always had a good head for business and when he graduated from college his first job was with a mortgage company. Over the years he experienced a series of promotions and so stayed with the company. At age 40 he looked at his life and saw that he was a mortgage lender by default. It was a career he had fallen into, not one he had chosen, and it bored him much of the time. That boredom translated into a generalized feeling of fatigue that he fought against nearly every day. When he asked himself what he really wanted to do, what he felt passionate about, he knew in a moment that he wanted to run a hardware store. Will Dennis be able to let go of his good-paying position to follow his passion? He is already taking some small steps. He has noticed that whenever he thinks about the hardware store, or takes any action in that direction, his energy level immediately increases. So he has started to plan ways to involve himself in the hardware business.

When you become clear about your personal mission, you don't necessarily walk in to your boss and hand him or her your resignation! Identification is only the first step in the process. At this step you're looking inside for your personal purpose. Once this is done, you can move on to planning and goal-setting, informational interviewing, résumé writing, and market analysis. For more information on this process, see *Finding Your Purpose* by Barbara Braham.[9]

Sneaking stress, whether it's dissatisfaction with your work, ageism, sexism, racism, or strained interpersonal relationships, is not resolved quickly. It continues day after day and week after week, wearing you down just as surely as water running over a rock eventually wears it away. As Josh Billings writes, "It's the little things that fret and worry us; you can dodge an elephant, but not a fly."

Take, for example, the cases of Jerry and Mildred. Both of them are suffering from sneaking chronic stress, although for different reasons.

Jerry has worked for the same manufacturing company for the past seven years as a purchasing agent. He enjoyed the work until about a year ago when he got a new boss. Now it seems he just can't do anything that pleases this man. For everything he does right, his boss criticizes three other things. Jerry has tried to talk with him, but they just don't seem to communicate. Now Jerry hates to see the boss coming and feels tired and irritable at the end of the day. Just the thought of Monday mornings has started to make him feel depressed on Sunday afternoons.

Mildred works in the accounting department of a small chemical company and is also under chronic stress. Eighteen months ago her company was bought out by a larger, multinational corporation. Since then, her firm has been in constant turmoil. First there was uncertainty about who would be laid off. Then the new management arrived with their own ideas about how to do things. The accounting procedures have changed four times since the buyout! There seems to be no stability anymore, and she wonders how much longer she can cope with the situation.

Both Jerry and Mildred are beginning to experience the effects of chronic stress, which, over a prolonged period of time, sneaks up on you in the form of symptoms. Rather than a specific incident, it is the buildup of small demands that result in chronic stress. You may not realize how deeply the stress is affecting you until you are suddenly faced with symptoms like fatigue or Jerry's Sunday depressions.

Ask yourself these questions to see if you have sneaking stress.

1. Do you feel tired much of time, even after a good night's rest?
2. Have you felt less positive about life recently, as though things won't work out in your favor?
3. Do you notice yourself feeling irritable much of the time?
4. Do you notice yourself feeling frustrated much of the time?
5. Does it seem harder and harder to get started on your *To Do* list each day?
6. Do you sometimes wonder when someone will notice that lately you haven't been as productive as you usually are?
7. Do you notice that, although you aren't sick, you don't really feel well?

The more yes answers you give to the above questions, the more likely that stress is starting to sneak up on you. Sneaking stress leads to burnout. If you're experiencing sneaking stress, you will find the life-change techniques in this book especially helpful.

Self-Imposed Stress

You want to believe that the stress you experience is coming from the outside: your job, the people you work with, the economy, and so on. Although these outside events may serve as triggers, the stress actually originates on the inside. In other words, you do it to yourself. You may not realize that some of the habits you've developed over the years are at the root of the stress you feel. While it isn't always easy to change your personal habits, it can be done. This is one place where you *do* have control. One of the most important habits is to gain control of your thoughts. Stress results when you lose control, give up control, or if you've never had control of your thoughts. In other words, which thoughts do you focus on? What thoughts get your attention? Which thoughts do you add to and thereby strengthen? Which thoughts do you let go? If you don't control your consciousness, you won't be able to control your stress.

Are you a worrier? If so, you're creating your own stress. You find ways to upset yourself. There is always something to worry about. Will there be an accident on the way to work? Is your work good enough? What do other people think about you? Will you meet the deadline? Worry keeps you in the past or the future instead of the present. The list goes on. None of these situations need to be stressful, but worrying about them makes them so. Worry is mental abuse. You need to stop doing it if you want to reduce your stress. If you're a worrier, you aren't in control of your thoughts. You'll learn techniques to help you stop worrying in Chapter 3.

Perhaps you're a workaholic, routinely working over 50 hours per week. You arrive at work before the sun rises and stay long after dark. You feel guilty about the number of times you've let family and friends down by promising to attend some function and then arriving late or not at all. You probably have a sinking feeling that no matter how hard you work or how many hours you put in, you keep falling farther and farther behind. You live the paradox: The faster I go, the behinder I get.

Are you a negative thinker? You want things to work out for the best, but you can't help but see the potential problems. You try to be cautious and consequently see only the worst in other people. Your life may be filled with fears—from fear of failure to fear of success.

Do you procrastinate? Often, stress comes when you feel under time pressure. Putting things off can create a last-minute time pressure. In addition, most people who procrastinate simultaneously beat up on themselves for this negative habit. This, in turn, lowers self-esteem.

If you generally struggle with feelings of low self-esteem, you increase the chances that you'll engage in a whole cluster of behaviors commonly referred to as Type A behavior. You'll learn more about Type A and Type B behavior in Chapter 4.

Perfectionism and unrealistic expectations are two more personal traits that cause stress. You are unique, not perfect. Strive for excellence in what you do. Businesses today are dedicated to continuous quality improvement, not perfection. That's good advice for you. Rather than trying to be perfect and creating unrealistic expectations for yourself, strive to continually develop yourself. This attitude will produce better results for you with less stress.

Worry, workaholism, negative thinking, procrastination, low self-esteem, and perfectionism are just some of the traits that cluster together to form a personality that feels stress in even the most relaxed situations. In reality, it is not outside events but how you interpret these events that causes you stress. The good news is that self-imposed stress is 100 percent within your control! If you created it, you can eliminate it!

Physical Environment Stress

Although there are many different stressors, you probably don't usually think of the physical environment as one of them. Thus, you may have overlooked it as the cause of your symptoms. That's what happened to Chuck, who worked in the data-entry department of a large direct-mail company.

Chuck just couldn't understand why he was having so much lower back pain. He couldn't recall any injury to his back. He bought a new mattress, and that didn't help. He talked to friends who suggested it was stress. That didn't make sense to him, though, because he loved his work and his marriage was terrific. After taking over-the-counter medications for several months, he decided to seek medical advice. The culprit was identified quickly. Chuck worked at a desktop computer all day, and the chair was the cause of the problem. Added to that was the intensity with which Chuck worked, often hours at a time without even a stretch break. A new chair and regular breaks solved the problem.

Let's look at another example—a woman who worked in the collections department of the attorney general's office.

For the past two weeks, Aisha had been coming home irritable and edgy. Usually delighted to see the children, she had been short-tempered and easily upset, constantly yelling at them: "Be quiet!" "Stop all that noise!" "Go play in the other room!" It wasn't until after she and her husband talked that she realized how much the construction near her office had affected her. The sound of jack hammers had been nearly constant for two weeks. Aisha had to yell to talk to co-workers, and she had difficulty concentrating. When she left the office, she craved quiet and solitude.

Noise and uncomfortable furniture are just two environmental stressors. A smoke-filled office can cause headaches; air pollution of any type can cause irritability or physical complaints; and intense heat or extreme cold can affect your mood and energy.

Common Work Stressors

Take a moment now to jot down the kind of stressors you experience at work.

Desired work changes _____

Unexpected work changes _____

Sneaking stressors _____

Self-imposed stressors _____

Physical environment stressors _____

You might want to know if the stresses *you* experience are common to others. The most frequently cited causes of job stress are time pressures (multiple priorities, deadlines, and scheduling); inadequate support; interpersonal conflict with a boss or subordinate; fear of failure; unclear expectations; and change.

The next section will give you an opportunity to complete a questionnaire to assess your current level of work stress.

Braham's Work Stress Inventory

Figure 1–1 is an instrument that lets you see the relative severity of your work stress. Take a moment now to look through this list and put a check mark beside any situation you have experienced in the past year. A check mark beside any of the items in Section A indicates sneaking stress. The severity of your stress is based on how long you have been in this situation. Remember that these chronic stressors are the most difficult to manage. For the items in Section B, a total of 10 or more checks indicates high work stress, a total of 5 to 9 checks indicates moderate work stress, and a total of 5 or fewer checks indicates low work stress.

FIGURE 1–1
Braham's Work Stress Inventory

Check any of the following experiences you have had in the last 12 months.

Section A

_____ Fired

_____ Laid off

_____ Quit without another job

_____ Company reorganization (buyout or merger)

_____ Company experienced major growth (doubled in size)

_____ Ongoing conflict with boss

_____ Ongoing conflict with peers

_____ Ongoing conflict with subordinates

_____ Company lost major client or source of funding

_____ Company introduced new technology

_____ Company introduced new management approach, e.g., total quality management (TQM)

_____ Total

Section B

_____ Major disappointment (not selected for promotion, project not funded or canceled, etc.)

_____ No room for advancement

_____ Highly political environment

_____ Fired an employee

_____ Laid off an employee

_____ Multiple bosses

_____ No control over daily work schedule

_____ Bored at work

_____ Changed bosses

_____ Manage multiple projects

_____ Give speeches/presentations to higher levels of management

_____ Promoted

FIGURE 1–1 *(concluded)*

_____ Demoted
_____ Received a negative performance appraisal
_____ Gave a negative performance appraisal
_____ Transferred
_____ Travel regularly (8+ days per month)
_____ Made a major wrong decision
_____ Change in senior management
_____ Job description changed
_____ Company moved
_____ Work overtime regularly
_____ Unclear expectations
_____ Face frequent (daily or weekly) deadlines
_____ Cyclical heavy workload (budgets, tax season, etc.)
_____ Changing priorities
_____ Regular customer contact
_____ Company lost money over past year
_____ Major change in your industry (government regulations,
            competition, etc.)
_____ Total

The greater the number of items you check, the higher your risk for experiencing symptoms associated with the stress. By practicing the ideas in this book to CALM down, you can manage those stressors and make them work for you.

UNDERSTANDING STRESS

Now that you know what causes work stress—just about anything—let's define exactly what you're dealing with. Hans Seyle, a pioneer in stress research, defined stress as "the nonspecific response of the body to any demand."[10] As we have just seen, that demand can be desired, unexpected, sneaking, self-imposed, or environmental. Why is it, then, that one person feels stress in a particular situation while another person feels completely relaxed?

The Role of Perception

Bill is the director of finance at a large lawn-care company. He is often asked to make presentations to senior management and the board of directors. Whenever one of these presentations is scheduled, he starts to worry about it. He has always felt uncomfortable in front of groups, and even though he is prepared, he sometimes goes "blank" in the middle of his talk. Because of his fear, he often rushes through his presentation and notices later that he left out a key point. His boss has told him that he could advance further in the company if he would develop his presentation skills. So far Bill hasn't wanted to take any classes or do anything that requires him to do any more speaking than he already does.

Brian, on the other hand, loves to speak. He is the director of franchises for the company that employs Bill. Brian has always been a bit of a "ham" and loves to be in front of a group. He speaks easily from a brief outline and welcomes the opportunity to get in front of a group whenever he can. He likes to tease Bill because Brian can't understand what is so scary about giving a speech.

In any situation, some people see a threat and feel stressed, while others see opportunity and feel excited. The mystic Rumi wrote, "What a piece of bread looks like depends on whether you're hungry or not." Nothing is, except as you live it. You decide, based on your perception, if something is pleasant or unpleasant, stressful or not.

Bill felt threatened about speaking, whereas Brian felt challenged. Situations in and of themselves are neutral: how you perceive them affects how you feel. In Chapter 3 you will take an in-depth look at how you can control stress through thinking and perception. For now, what's important is that you recognize the connection between perception and stress. Let's say that stress is the nonspecific response of the body to any demand *you perceive as a threat.*

Control versus Controlling

One of the most critical areas of perception is *control.* Do you believe you have control of your life? The more you feel in control of what happens to you, the healthier you will be. People who feel they have control of their lives, their jobs, their time, and so on experience less stress than people who don't feel in control. This is why some low-level employees feel more stress than senior managers. While it is true that senior managers have greater responsibility and make more frequent and far-reaching decisions, they are also more in control of their schedules, the projects they work on, and the kind of help they will use. A receptionist can't even go to the bathroom when she wants to—she has to wait for a relief receptionist! First-line supervisors do what they are told by management, respond to the needs of their employees, make few decisions, and often have their days controlled by someone else's schedule. Fortunately for managing stress, this is beginning to change as more companies move toward total quality management (TQM) and empowered workplaces. A key component of TQM is that people closest to the work need to make decisions concerning that work. As employees at all levels in the organization feel more control over their work, their stress level will be reduced.

According to the National Institute for Occupational Safety and Health, among the most stressful jobs are licensed practical nurse, quality control inspector, public relations specialist, computer programmer, and bank teller—all positions in which employees don't feel in charge of their jobs. A research study conducted by Northwestern National Life in 1992 confirms these findings. In their study of 1,299 full-time employees in private-sector companies across the country, they found that when supervisors delegated control to the employee on how to do the work, 70 percent of those employees reported low levels of job stress.[11]

An important distinction needs to be made between exercising control and being controlling. Csikszentmihalyi in *Flow* writes, "It is not possible to experience a feeling of control unless one is willing to give up the safety of protective routines. Only when a doubtful outcome is at stake, and one is able to influence that outcome, can a person really know whether she is in control."[12] Being controlling is a negative behavior used most often by people who feel they do not have control. They want things done their way and on their schedule. Thus a payroll clerk who feels she doesn't have much control over her work becomes controlling with other employees. She might establish an arbitrary rule that payroll sheets must be turned in by 10:00 A.M. on Wednesday. If a sheet is turned in one minute late, she refuses to process it. Being controlling is a form of rigidity, and people who are rigid can break (i.e., burnout).

Exercising control, on the other hand, recognizes that you are not in control. Forces outside of you are in control. Nonetheless, you have tremendous capability to exercise your personal strengths and resources to respond most appropriately to the situation. The greater your own sense of control, the more powerful you feel. Ironically, this leads to less controlling behavior. If you believe you can handle a situation, you don't need to make it happen your way. You are free to relax and respond to whatever occurs. Here's the paradox: to gain control, relinquish control. Thus, to feel good, you balance taking action with the knowledge that you can't control everything.

Let's look at the case of Toni, who supervised a department of sales associates who monthly turned in expenses for reimbursement. Toni trusted her people and asked them to submit at the end of each month a total of their expenses, which she approved for payment. If there was an unusual expense of more than $25, she requested a receipt. When Toni was promoted, Darlene moved into her position. Darlene wanted to be sure no one took advantage of her and immediately implemented a new procedure requiring a receipt to document every expense. Morale plummeted among the sales associates who felt controlled and who often ate on the road at fast-food restaurants where they didn't always remember to ask for a receipt. Under the new supervisor, many expenses were not reimbursed because the sales associate simply forgot to get a receipt for $2.19. Darlene thought she was doing great. She was on top of things. Eventually she got exactly what she asked for. People did only what they were directly asked to do. Sales associates stopped going the "extra mile" for customers or the company. Within three months Darlene was complaining of how much stress she was under. She didn't see how her behavior was the source of that stress.

Toni had exercised her control by setting limits for her sales associates. Darlene tried to control their behavior. The sales associates would have done anything for Toni because she exercised the same style in all of her interactions with her staff. After Darlene came on board, the company couldn't understand why there was such a motivation problem with the sales department. Are you more like Toni or Darlene?

You'll see another example of the paradox in action in Chapter 5 when you read about relaxation techniques. You cannot *make* or *will* yourself to relax. The harder you try to control the relaxation response, the more anxious and stressed you will become. The only way to relax is to relinquish control over your body and *allow* it to relax.

Sometimes you have no control over a situation. However, people who feel they have control of their lives realize they always have control over their *responses* to the situations. It is this belief that buoys some people, while others sink in exactly the same situations. In psychology this concept is called *locus of control*. In research studies, people with an external locus of control (i.e., they feel they are controlled by outside events and other people) suffered from feelings of powerlessness and increased their stress. In contrast, subjects with an internal locus of control (i.e., people who felt they could exercise some control over themselves in any situation) perceived themselves as more powerful and suffered from less stress. An external locus of control can lead to learned helplessness. A well-known example of this comes from circus elephants. When the elephants are young, they are tied to a heavy chain that they cannot move. Later when they become adults, they can be tied to a stake that they could pull up from the ground with little or no effort; but none of them do. Why not? Because they've learned that they can't control their environment. They no longer exercise their control. So it is with human beings. If some limits are set on you in one situation in your life, say, your childhood, it is easy for you to assume that those conditions will always exist. You may not make any efforts to change them later when you could exercise control over your situation. If you've sat through a meeting where people were asked their opinion and made no response, or if you've heard responses like "I don't care," "It doesn't matter to me," or "Do whatever you want," you've observed learned helplessness in action.

Sometimes you give away your control. For example, if you are asked to volunteer for an extra project, and rather than say no, thereby controlling your own time, you reluctantly agree and complain to others that you had no choice, you gave away your control. Giving away your control results in double stress: first, the lack of control, and second, the time pressure.

One theme that runs throughout this book is the importance of exercising control whenever you can—control of the situation, if possible, and control of your response to the situation, if you cannot control the situation.

Eustress and Distress

Not all stress is bad. Most people need a certain amount of stress to feel motivated. Who hasn't said, "I work well under pressure"? In fact, insufficient stress is stressful! Think back to a time when you felt bored in your job— not challenged or stimulated. Remember how the time used to drag? If you think about it, you will probably recall feeling stress.

Distress occurs when you are underloaded or overloaded with stress. Eustress occurs when you have enough stress to feel motivated and challenged and to work at peak productivity. Csikszentmihalyi in his book Flow writes, "Enjoyment appears at the boundary between boredom and anxiety—when the challenges are just balanced with the person's capacity to act."[13] The boundary between distress and eustress is where growth takes place. It's the point of optimal experience and productivity. Picture a bell-shaped curve. Eustress is sandwiched between the underload or overload of distress. This phenomena is called the firehouse syndrome. Fire fighters are either sitting in the firehouse waiting for something to happen or racing to a fire—underload or overload. Accountants, retailers, and construction workers are also prone to the firehouse syndrome because of the cyclical nature of their jobs (tax season, holidays or sales, and weather). Anyone faced with seasonal or cyclical work confronts this problem.

The cycle is also played out in different ways at different points in the life cycle. When you are young, the demands on you are fewer and your capacity to respond to them is high. As you approach middle age, managing stress becomes more difficult because there are more demands with higher pressure for performance, although your capacity may remain the same as in youth or it may begin to drop off. Later in life there is less capacity and also less demand. Therefore, the most difficult time for managing stress is during the middle years.

The risk for distress during the middle years is further compounded by lifestyle choices. Bad habits developed in the 20s and early 30s (such as smoking, drinking, poor eating habits, sedentary lifestyle) have a cumulative effect that isn't seen for 10 to 20 years—until midlife. The combination of unwise lifestyle choices and stress leads to symptoms that aren't seen until the middle years.

Fight-or-Flight Response

When the body has a demand placed on it or perceives a threat, it responds physically with the *fight-or-flight response*. This response served human beings well long ago when they encountered physical threats like wild tigers, which they had to run from or fight. Today when you need to call a dissatisfied customer on the phone, your body reacts with the same fight-or-flight response. Unfortunately, this is not a situation in which you can fight or run away. Instead, you need to deal calmly with customers; you need to blend and flow with the situation. Your body, not knowing this, proceeds with the fight-or-flight response anyway.

Once a threat is perceived, an alarm goes off throughout the body. The heart rate increases, and blood is drawn away from the extremities and concentrated in the deep muscle groups. Also, the pupils dilate, the jaw clenches, and adrenaline, sugar, and fats pour into the bloodstream. Breathing shifts from slow, deep, diaphragmatic breathing to shallow chest breathing. These mechanisms work well when one is in a life-threatening situation; however, when one needs to return a customer's phone call, activation of the fight-or-flight response will wear out the body unnecessarily.

It's a little like driving your car. If you continually drive with the emergency brake on, you never will have the power or speed of which your car is capable. After a while, you will burn out your brakes. It is equally possible to burn out your body.

At the Indianapolis 500, the race cars make a pit stop after about 40 laps. All the tires are replaced, the radiator is cleaned, the suspension is adjusted, and the car is refueled. When the race is over, the entire engine is replaced. Although many people drive their bodies like race cars, it is not so easy to schedule a "pit stop" during which the heart is replaced, the muscles are repaired, or the stomach is relined!

Nearly 75 percent of all illness is believed to be caused or worsened by unmanaged stress.[14] When you're under stress, the immune system is suppressed, thus increasing your vulnerability to illness. An entirely new field of study called psychoneuroimmunology has emerged to study the interaction of the mind, the nervous system, and the immune system.

Are You Headed for Burnout?

Burnout follows a prolonged period of high stress in which the body remains continuously in the fight or flight state. It's characterized by depression; a loss of meaning; and impaired health, work, and personal relationships. There are four early warning signs that you're approaching burnout. The first is busyness. Are you too busy? In other words, do you live your life according to the word *Next?* If you go through your days preparing *To Do* lists and then rushing to cross off one item after another, yet end the day wondering why you did what you did, that's an early signal of impending burnout.

When you get caught in the trap of busyness, you sacrifice presence. That means that although your body shows up at a meeting or an appointment, the rest of you is somewhere else; you left it at the previous meeting, or it's already at some future event. You may go through the motions, but you're not there emotionally, mentally, or spiritually. Consequently, you miss the richness of life. Everything begins to feel the same. There isn't any difference between this customer and the last one. You've heard all the same problems before; nothing seems fresh or alive anymore—because you aren't. Presence is the way you connect with another person when you communicate. When you sacrifice your presence for expediency, or to get through your *To Do* list, you've taken the first step down the path of sacrificing your Self.

As busyness continues, you will become so caught up in the treadmill of tasks to be done that you'll almost imperceptibly move into the second warning sign of approaching burnout, and that's postponing joy. The first few times you tell your family you have to work late, or you're just going in for a few hours on Saturday to get caught up, you'll feel that you're missing something. But quickly, you'll tell yourself that responding to a few more letters or reviewing a trade magazine is a much better use of your time than following through on your exercise program or seeing friends or volunteering in the community. You'll promise yourself that you'll come back to these activities later when you aren't under so much pressure. But if you're headed for burnout, later never comes. Postponing time for joy and fun, activities that have the potential to offer you self-renewal, becomes the norm and not the exception.

Once you stop caring for yourself in favor of the almighty tasks to be done, you're vulnerable to the third sign of burnout. That's living life according to *have-to's* and *shoulds*. Your expectations of yourself will have mushroomed. No longer able to discern the important from the unimportant, you will increasingly feel compelled to do everything. You will become overly sensitive to what others think. No longer able to please yourself, you'll try to please the others in the world—an impossible task.

This leads to the fourth warning sign of burnout—loss of perspective. Now everything feels urgent and important. You're surrounded by crisis and demands. Vacations are postponed, or if you go, you call in every day to check on things. A typographical error becomes a catastrophe. Everything seems to be a fire that only you can douse. You've lost your sense of humor, your ability to go with the flow, and your ability to adapt and problem-solve. To your co-workers you appear desperate and overextended. They try to get you to take some time off. Increasingly you find yourself suffering from physical or other ailments. It's time to take some ameliorative action. But having reached the point of burnout, you find your energy level depleted, your mental attitude negative, and your motivation nonexistent. Coming out of burnout to self-renewal is a long, slow process. You don't have to wait for burnout to take action. By learning to manage your

stress following the principles in this book, you can prevent burnout.

SYMPTOMS OF STRESS

When you don't manage your stress, your body experiences the fight-or-flight response over and over, and you
begin to experience symptoms. Just what those symptoms
are varies from person to person. Everyone has a "weak
link," a vulnerable place that tends to break down when
you're exposed to repeated stress. You may be affected in
any one or some combination of the following ways.

Physical Symptoms

It's often not until your body develops symptoms that
you decide to take action to reduce stress. In 1990, $666.2
billion was spent on health care in the United States, according to the world almanac, and much of that was a
direct result of unmanaged stress.

Look over the list below, and check off any physical
symptoms you are experiencing.

_____ Headaches
_____ Sleep disorders (e.g., insomnia, oversleeping,
          early morning awakening)
_____ Backaches (especially lower back pain)
_____ Clenching the jaws or grinding the teeth
_____ Constipation
_____ Diarrhea and colitis
_____ Skin rashes
_____ Muscle aches (especially neck and shoulders)
_____ Indigestion or ulcers
_____ Hypertension or heart attack
_____ Excessive perspiration
_____ Appetite change

_____ Fatigue or loss of energy
_____ Increase in accidents
_____ (Add your own)

Emotional Symptoms

These are the symptoms that may lead you to a counselor's office. Check off the symptoms that you experience.

_____ Anxiety or worry
_____ Depression or crying easily
_____ Mood swings
_____ Irritability
_____ Nervousness
_____ Lowered self-esteem or feelings of insecurity
_____ Increased sensitivity or feeling easily hurt
_____ Angry outbursts
_____ Aggression or hostility
_____ Feeling emotionally drained or burned out
_____ (Add your own)

Intellectual Symptoms

In the following example, you will see the impact that stress can have on intellectual functioning.

Carol couldn't understand what was wrong with Karen. Karen had always been an excellent worker, but this past week had been a disaster. As office manager, Karen was responsible for a variety of tasks that Carol had stopped monitoring long ago. Suddenly Carol found herself involved. The bank deposit wasn't added properly, and there was a call from the bank. The Federal Express packages destined for locations across the country all had the same address on them. A grant that had to be copied in triplicate and sent to three different agencies had pages missing. Karen began to seek Carol's advice on routine decisions she had always made. Worst of all, when Carol talked to Karen, she was faced with a blank stare that left her wondering if Karen was listening.

Karen was experiencing personal problems, and try as she might to leave them at home, they came to work with her. In her case, the stress showed up in the office as intellectual symptoms.

Look at the list below and check any symptoms you have.

_____ Trouble concentrating

_____ Difficulty making decisions

_____ Forgetfulness

_____ Confusion

_____ Poor memory and recall

_____ Excessive daydreaming

_____ Preoccupation with a single thought or idea

_____ Loss of sense of humor

_____ Decreased productivity

_____ Lower quality of work

_____ Increased number of errors

_____ Poor judgment

_____ (Add your own)

Interpersonal Symptoms

Stress can also affect your relationships with others, both on the job and at home. Strained work relationships quickly become one of the chronic stressors identified earlier in this chapter. Now, in addition to the original stressor—perhaps changing technology in the office—there is the compounding factor of an unpleasant interpersonal situation. It is unlikely you'll get support to cope with the original stress if you damage your relationships with those who could support you.

Look through the list below and check off any symptoms you are experiencing.

_____ Inappropriate distrust of others

_____ Blaming others

_____ Missing appointments or canceling them on short notice

_____ Faultfinding and verbal attacking

_____ Overly defensive attitude

_____ Giving others the "silent treatment"

_____ (Add your own)

The more items you have checked on the previous four lists, the higher your stress level.

The first step in gaining control of stress is awareness. Until you notice when and how stress affects you, you cannot manage it. Look back over the symptom lists you have just completed. How does stress affect you? Can you recognize the early warning signals, or do you wait for symptoms? How intense are your symptoms? How often do they appear? As you become more attuned to your personal stress response, you can apply the CALM model more effectively.

THE CALM MODEL

The remainder of this book outlines a four-step process called the CALM model, which can help you manage the work stress you experience. You'll be pleased to know that the model is equally effective with the stress in your personal life. Each step will show you ways to take control of your life so that stress works *for* you and not *against* you. The model is based on the premise that to manage your stress may cause short-term pain as you engage in new and sometimes unfamiliar habits. However, the benefit is a long-term gain as the new behaviors create a healthier lifestyle for you. You may be tempted to look for short-term gain, a quick fix to make you feel better now. Sadly, most short-term gains create long-term pain.

Don't Be Deceived by a "Short-Term Fix"

There is a big difference between *managing* stress and *coping* with stress. When you manage stress, you make it work for you; that is eustress. You can use the skills described in this book to monitor your stress level so stress does not become *dis*tress. You'll learn to exercise control to take charge of stressful situations and your reactions to them. Most stress management efforts are long-term solutions to the stressors you experience.

In contrast, when you cope with stress, you're applying a short-term fix. You look for ways to make the immediate pain go away without necessarily looking for ways to resolve the underlying causes. Unfortunately, many of the short-term solutions (*copers*) turn into long-term stressors. For example, if you use alcohol to unwind from a stressful day, you may feel an immediate sense of relief. However, if that coper is used continually, it can become another problem—alcoholism. On the other hand, if you choose to manage your stress, you'll use an exercise program instead of alcohol to relax and unwind. This long-term strategy builds your resistance to stress and doesn't just hide it.

Most people have used short-term solutions like drugs, alcohol, a shopping spree, faultfinding, taking a day off, blaming, eating, smoking, or denial from time to time. However, if this is the only way you handle stress, your health and your relationships are bound to suffer.

There is a better solution than short-term fixes: to *manage* stress with the CALM approach.

The Model

Learning to be CALM is more than a set of techniques; it's a philosophy about how you're going to live your life. Stress management is ultimately lifestyle management. When you decide to manage your stress, you're making a decision about the quality of your life—emotionally, physically, and spiritually. You can learn to CALM down using the simple, easy-to-understand model shown in Figure 1–2. As you can see, CALM isn't a short-term fix; it's a long-term stress management plan. The only difficult thing is making the commitment to implement it.

The first step, C, is to change the situation when you can. Chapter 2 explains the questions you can ask yourself to see if change is possible, then gives you several skills you can use to implement the change. Changing the situation is a long-term strategy that is an alternative to the usual attempt to "be strong and try harder." If you change the situation, you may succeed in eliminating the stress altogether. This first step is an empowering one that restores to you a feeling of control over your life.

Chapter 3 describes the second step, A: accept the things you cannot change. There are situations you cannot control. Learn how to accept them without anger and how to keep your thinking positive. Acceptance is a powerful strategy that helps you move from the fight-or-flight response into the flow state. This step helps you recognize that when you can't control the situation, you can control your response. Your ability to accept what is will help you stay present to your life. Presence prevents burnout.

The third step, L, is to let go. In Chapter 4 you'll explore what you hold on to and how that can lead to tension and

FIGURE 1–2
The CALM Model

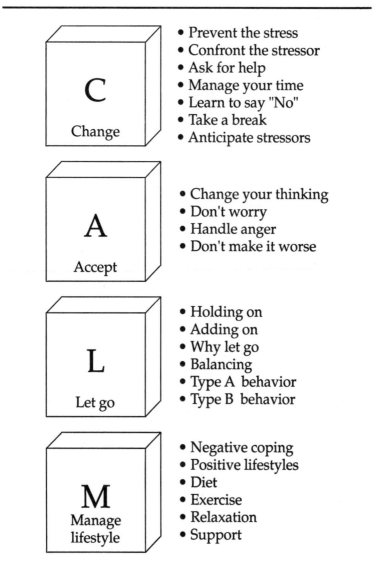

C — Change
- Prevent the stress
- Confront the stressor
- Ask for help
- Manage your time
- Learn to say "No"
- Take a break
- Anticipate stressors

A — Accept
- Change your thinking
- Don't worry
- Handle anger
- Don't make it worse

L — Let go
- Holding on
- Adding on
- Why let go
- Balancing
- Type A behavior
- Type B behavior

M — Manage lifestyle
- Negative coping
- Positive lifestyles
- Diet
- Exercise
- Relaxation
- Support

stress. You'll learn how to let go of such things as your unrealistic expectations, negative belief systems, and the self-imposed stress that only makes matters worse. Letting go is a powerful tool that works emotionally, mentally, spiritually, and physically. This chapter will help you unleash the power in the paradox—to gain control, relinquish control. To hold on to control when you can't change the situation leads to your becoming controlling. And that escalates stress.

Finally, Chapter 5 will cover the fourth step, M: manage your lifestyle. This step gives you a number of ways in which you can start raising your resistance to tomorrow's stressors *today*, through exercise, diet, relaxation, and emotional support. You'll also learn a variety of relaxation techniques you can put into practice immediately. These strategies actually increase your capacity to respond to life's demands. You may be unable to control the stressors in your life, but you can take action to increase your ability to respond to them. When you first start jogging, you might only be able to run one block. But with practice and committed effort you can increase your capacity until you're able to run a mile or better. That's what the last step of the model is about. Today you may only be able to cope with one or two stressors in your life. As you learn to better manage your lifestyle, you'll increase your capacity until you can handle three or four or more stressors.

SUMMARY

Stress can be caused by change (desired or unexpected), sneaking stressors, your personal traits, or the physical environment.

Whether you experience a particular situation as stressful or not is determined by your perception of the situation. You can reduce your stress by perceiving situations as a challenge rather than as a threat. If you are overloaded or underloaded with stress, you are likely to develop symptoms. These may show up physically, emotionally, interpersonally, intellectually, or in some combination of these. If you don't take action to manage your stress when the symptoms first appear or before, they can escalate into burnout.

There is something you can do about stress. You can learn to CALM down by applying the model in this book. Learning to be CALM is more than a bag of tricks. It's a philosophy that will impact the quality of your life.

Chapter Two

The C of CALM: Change the Situation

You probably become aware of stress when it is acute. Your muscles tense, you experience some of the symptoms discussed in Chapter 1, or you feel anxious. At this point the typical response is to try to cope with the stress.

PREVENT THE STRESS

There is a better first step. Before you jump into coping with the situation, stop and allow yourself a few minutes to think. Take several deep breaths to relax and clear your mind. One technique you can use to do this is the Quieting Reflex described in Chapter 5. Then ask yourself this question: Is there anything I can do to change the situation to avoid or reduce the stress I am feeling?

It may help to have a piece of paper handy so you can write down any ideas that come to mind. Then after you list all your ideas, you can go back through the list and decide which of them, if any, are workable. This brief time-out lets you brainstorm strategies to manage the stress rather than just coping with it.

The process also gives you a sense of control. No longer powerless or helpless against the stress, you now actively decide the best way to respond. Too often people give away their power at this early stage and then feel victimized. The secret of this first step of the model is to take responsibility for changing a situation so it is less stressful for you. You empower yourself by taking responsibility for your life. You don't wait for someone else to change, or hope that they will do something different so that you feel less stress. You become an active player in your own life instead of a passive victim.

Anthony Robbins, in his book *Awaken the Giant Within*, describes three specific beliefs about responsibility you need to hold to make changes in your life.[1] First, you must believe that a change is needed. Second, you need to believe that you are the person who can change your life. And last, you need to believe that change is possible. Without these three core beliefs, you will find it difficult to practice what is being suggested as the first step to CALM down.

Look at the case of Jerome, who works in the accounting department of a hospital. Jerome felt overwhelmed. He had a major budget review due at 4:00 P.M. He had been working on the project for the past week and still had about four hours of work in front of him. The problem was that he didn't have four hours available. He had a supervisory conference scheduled in the morning and a committee meeting scheduled in the afternoon. He coped by skipping lunch and taking some of his work to the committee meeting. The meetings usually didn't demand his full attention anyway.

Jerome did not take the time to think through his situation. He didn't act; instead he *reacted* and, in the process, increased his level of stress. If he had used the CALM model, he would first have asked himself the following empowering questions. By so doing, he could have gained control of his situation.

SEVEN EMPOWERING QUESTIONS

Can Someone Else Do It?

Who else can help? Is there anyone who could attend the meeting for him? Could anyone else finish the budget review for him? Could part of the budget review be done by someone else, thereby reducing the time Jerome would need to spend on it?

Can someone else do it? is a question you can ask yourself when you start to feel stressed. Who else can help you? Is there someone in your department who could give a helping hand? Or is there someone in another department in the company with a lower workload who might be able to help you? Sometimes it can be more cost-effective and less stressful to hire a temporary worker to assist with a special project. You may be able to use a temporary worker to handle the routine tasks while you focus on the special project.

Embedded in this question is your willingness to ask for help. Some people find this difficult to do. They mistakenly think that if they can't do everything, they aren't good enough, or that there is something wrong with them. If this is true for you, you may want to consider building your self-esteem. If you have a perfectionistic streak, you may be unwilling to ask for help because no one else will do it "your way." Is your way worth your health?

Using this first empowering question is also difficult because it may mean you need to say no. Many people find it difficult to say no because they want to be liked and accepted by others. They fear a loss of approval if they say no. Consequently, if you fail to ask the first empowering question, you may find yourself overcommitted and feeling stressed.

Yes is a word that seems to lead to more yeses. Remember, when you say yes to something, you're saying no to everything else. In other words, if you say yes to working overtime, you're saying no to time with your family or time for yourself. Too often, people don't take the time to assess what a yes really means. Here are six questions that Tom Speros, a family physician in North Carolina asks himself before using the word yes. You might try them before you say yes.

1. Is it worthwhile?
2. Am I willing to give it my best?
3. Am I uniquely qualified to accomplish the task or to contribute to its success?
4. Do I want to do it?
5. What will I have to sacrifice to accomplish the task?
6. Is the task more important than what will have to be given up?

Later in this chapter, you'll learn the five steps to follow if you decide you want to say no to a request.

Can Something Be Delayed?

Jerome assumed everything had to be done at once. He created even more stress for himself by trying to attend a meeting and work on his report at the same time. Most of us are less productive when we try to do two things at the same time, each of which requires our full attention. Jerome would have been wiser to think through the consequences of changing one of his deadlines. For example, could the budget review be delayed until the next morning? Could the supervisory conference be rescheduled for another day? Could the meeting be postponed? In Jerome's case, it is reasonable to assume he could delay the supervisory conference. This would give him at least one extra hour.

Do you set unrealistic expectations for yourself? If you do, this second empowering question may help you step out of the Superwoman or Superman complex. Befriend yourself! In today's fast-paced world of fax machines, cellular telephones, and sophisticated technology, everything may seem like an urgent priority that requires immediate attention. Also, with the rapid rate of change and speed of communications, it is easy to underestimate timelines and to overcommit results. Take desktop publishing as a simple example. Just a few years ago a typed newsletter was considered professional. Today, expectations have been raised. To be perceived as professional, the newsletter needs to be desktop-published with graphics, with different type styles and an artistic layout. It's easy to forget that this requires more time and not less time, despite the fact that your hardware and software are significantly faster and more sophisticated than in the past. Thus, today's fast pace and high technology have clouded our ability to discern what is urgent from what is parading as urgent. It is also more difficult to take the time to evaluate which new technologies save time, and which cost time.

Be realistic with yourself. When you're beginning to feel stress, ask yourself, "Can it be delayed?" This poem, written by Leslie Charles, president of TrainingWorks, Inc., can be a helpful reminder to keep your expectations of yourself in perspective. Remember, keeping your perspective helps prevent burnout.

Perspective

I don't have to have it all or be it all
I don't need to do it all or know it all
What I do need is to know who I am,

know what I want,
know what makes me happy
and know how to get my needs met.
If I can do that successfully,
all the rest will fall into place.

Can I Substitute Something Else?

Jerome might ask if he could submit a draft of his budget review rather than the final report. Perhaps he could give an overview with a final detailed written report to follow. Instead of attending the committee meeting, he might prepare a brief written summary of his opinions or suggestions and deliver these to the committee chair along with how he would like to vote on any known issues.

Perfectionists will find Can I substitute something else? a particularly difficult question. The reality is, most things don't need to be done perfectly. A phone call may be as effective as a letter. A teleconference may handle a problem as well as a meeting. A form letter may satisfactorily replace a personalized letter. Be on the lookout for ways to streamline your work. Your challenge is to apply the paradox that less is more. As demands increase and the personnel to meet those demands decreases—typical in the downsized workplaces of the 1990s—you need to become increasingly clear on what is your highest valued work. When your values are clear, you can stop spending precious time and energy on lower priority items. People who are successful in the 1990s will be clear on their personal and corporate values.

The process being suggested here is analogous to TQM. The essence of TQM is to find more efficient and effective ways to produce continuously improving quality products. You're after the same goal when it comes to managing stress. You're simultaneously looking for ways to reduce the stressors while increasing your capacity to respond to them. The question Can I substitute something else? does both. First you try to eliminate the stressor, and if that's not possible, you're going to reduce the energy you need to spend to respond to it.

One reminder if you tend to be a perfectionist: Perfection isn't possible for human beings. Another paradox is that we are perfect in our imperfection! To put the burden of perfectionism on yourself is to create unnecessary stress. Focus instead on your uniqueness. Separate yourself from others, not through perfection but through what makes you undeniably *you*.

Is It Essential?

What is the worst thing that could happen if Jerome doesn't do everything? How important is the committee meeting? Is it essential? Would it make much difference if he called and said he could not attend? What about the supervisory conference? If this is a weekly meeting, would it matter if he canceled, or is this the annual performance appraisal, which cannot be delayed? Who is the budget review for? What are the consequences if it is not complete? Is this a report to the senior vice president, or is this a progress report to his immediate supervisor?

This question is further pushing you to gain clarity about your values. You can probably do or have just about anything. The curse is that you can't have everything. What is of the greatest value to you and your company? When you stop trying to do everything, you can focus your efforts and reduce your stress.

This question will lead you to be more inner-directed instead of outer-directed. In other words, you will decide for yourself, based on your values, what is and what isn't essential. Without a high level of self-esteem, you will find it is easy to let other people's ideas of what is essential control your behavior. For example, there may be a meeting that your colleagues are attending after business hours that they think you, too, should attend. But you don't have the same goals and aspirations. You're tired and want to go work out at the gym. If you ask yourself Is it essential? and answer from your values, the answer will be no. But if you answer from the need to please others, your answer may well be yes, and you may end up feeling stressed.

There are some people who would guide you into how to manage your time to do both. The point here is not to be efficient before you are effective. Being effective means knowing if it is worth doing at all before you figure out how to do more of it faster.

Will a Job Aid Help?

Another question to consider is, Can I use any tools or training to help me do the job faster or more easily? Suppose Jerome was manually preparing for his budget several scenarios based on various percentages for salary increases. If he were using an electronic spreadsheet program, it would automatically make those calculations. Learning a new job aid might be more expensive and time-consuming in the short run than doing the calculations manually. However, if this is a task Jerome completes often, the long-term gains may exceed the short-term costs. To plunge ahead without thinking about this can keep Jerome perpetually stressed. By asking yourself this question, you may identify ways to reduce future stress, even though you cannot change the current stress.

Keep in mind that a job aid is a broad category. The most commonly thought-of job aids are technology or equipment. However, equally important as job aids are so-called soft aids such as training in interpersonal communication, enhancing listening skills, learning to manage time, and even this book on managing stress! Anything that increases your capacity to do the job can qualify as a job aid.

This empowering question is perhaps one of the most difficult because at the time you're feeling stressed, investing time to delegate or learn how to use a new piece of equipment or attend a course seems antithetical to reducing stress. But being CALM isn't just about feeling better today. It's a philosophy of making wise choices that will lead to long-term feelings of health and well-being. You are creating your future—including your future stress symptoms or their absence—with the choices you make today about how to respond to your stressors. Will you choose short-term pain for long-term gain?

Can the Stress Be Avoided?

All the questions thus far help you address the stress associated with a project, but what if the source of your stress is a person or a situation? In that case, ask yourself all the previous questions and one more: Can the stressful situation or person be avoided entirely? Imagine that you fight rush-hour traffic every morning and evening getting to and from work. You may cope with this now by trying to relax while you drive or perhaps by listening to audio cassettes. Using the CALM model, your first step is to evaluate the situation and ask yourself if the stress can be avoided. One solution might be leaving the house earlier, before the rush hour begins. You might also discuss with your boss the possibility of flextime, or you could consider public transportation. Perhaps you could join the increasing ranks of people who work at home. Any of these choices puts you in control and simultaneously lets you minimize the stress.

The stress for many people is the complexity of 20th century living. Out of this has sprung a whole movement toward voluntary simplicity. People are looking for ways to clarify their values and live their lives accordingly. One value that increasing numbers of people have come to hold is the paradox mentioned earlier: less is more. Thus, one component of voluntary simplicity is less consumption. That means less stress associated with storing, maintaining, caring, insuring, and worrying about *things*. Take just one product as an example—the automobile. Does your car ever create stress for you—driving it in rush hour traffic, trying to find a place to park it, servicing it, insuring it, protecting it, washing it, housing it? Some people are choosing to walk or use a bicycle or public transportation as one step toward simplifying their lives and reducing their stress. Many other examples abound. What you need to ask yourself is, What are the causes of stress for me? If any of them are related to your patterns of consumption, then avoiding the stress through a plan like voluntary simplicity might be an answer.

What if your boss is the source of the stress? The two of you simply don't get along, and whenever you are together you feel knots in your stomach. Can you avoid the situation? It's possible. You can request a transfer to another department or work on projects that give you independence and minimal contact with the boss. In a company with multiple shifts, you might change your hours. As a last option you can quit. It is not necessary to "make yourself sick" by staying in a negative situation. Recognizing your choices gives you more control. If you elect to stay and deal with the stressful relationship, you have minimized your stress simply by being in control of the decision. Then you do not feel stuck, trapped, or helpless. You have *chosen* to stay in the situation.

It is important to make a distinction here between *ignoring* a situation and actively avoiding it. Ignoring it is a passive and powerless response. It is like burying your head in the sand, hoping that when you look up the stress will have disappeared magically. This is just what it sounds like—magical thinking—and it leaves you feeling less in control and more stressed. Ignoring stressors does not make them go away. In contrast, avoidance is an *active* strategy in which the stressor is not hidden from view, but actually removed from your situation.

Finally, don't forget the power of planning to help you avoid stress. If you tend to procrastinate, then you have no doubt experienced situations in which stress was the result of waiting until the last minute. If you need to get something photocopied and wait until the day you need it, you'll put yourself into a stressful situation if the photocopier jams. If you take time to plan and make your copies a day or two in advance, a jammed photocopier becomes an inconvenience, not a stressor.

Can the Stressor Be Confronted?

If you cannot avoid the situation, ask yourself, Can I reduce the stress by confronting the situation or person? Imagine again that you are in conflict with your boss. You may not want to leave the situation because you love the job and enjoy working with colleagues. Before you decide to resign yourself to the situation the way it is and simply cope with it, use the CALM method. Why not confront the specific problems you have with your boss and attempt to resolve them? Please note that the word *confront* is not used to imply a hostile or adversarial approach. Rather, the word *confront* means to face the situation; you will address the stressor or stressful situation by taking action instead of playing the role of victim. If you can resolve the differences, you may reduce or eliminate the stress. In the next section you will learn the skills you can use to confront a person or situation.

The power of the previous seven questions is that they help you recognize your current situation and face squarely what you like and don't like about it. Then you can take charge of how you will respond to it.

After asking yourself these questions, you will have a list of possibilities before you. Let's look at Jerome's options to reduce his stress:

Don't attend the meeting—send someone else.

Don't attend the meeting—cancel.

Postpone the supervisory conference.

Cancel the supervisory conference.

Negotiate a later deadline for the budget review.

Submit a less comprehensive budget review than originally planned.

Combining several options from his list would make it possible for Jerome to meet the 4:00 P.M. deadline without unnecessary stress.

How often do you try to do everything, like Jerome did, with the result that you feel "stressed out"? Remember that once you are aware of feeling stress, the first step in managing it is to change the situation whenever you can.

Take a moment now to jot down a stressful situation you are facing. Then ask yourself the CALM questions.

Situation: _____

_____

_____

Can someone else do it? _____

_____

Can it be delayed? _____

_____

Can I substitute something else? _____

_____

Is it essential? _____

_____

Will a job aid help? _____

_____

Can the stress be avoided? _____

_____

Can the stressor be confronted? _____

_____

Action I will take: _____

CONFRONT THE STRESSOR

Deciding to change the situation is not enough to make it different. In fact, you haven't really made a decision until you empower it with action. You will need skills to take the actions you have chosen. The remainder of this chapter tells you how to develop the skills you need to manage stressful situations by changing them.

How to Confront Another Person

Most people feel uncomfortable when they think about confronting another person. This is because they don't have the tools to confront graciously and effectively. They erroneously assume that the only way to approach a disagreement or a different point of view is with anger or hostility. In fact, for some, confronting the situation would create more stress than merely coping with it. Part of your strategy will be to assess whether it is wiser for you to cope with a situation or confront it.

Before you decide to confront the other person, ask yourself these questions:

Who am I about to confront? Is it my boss? A co-worker? A friend?

What do I have to lose by expressing my feelings? What do I have to gain?

What is my emotional state? Am I angry? Upset? Calm? Concerned?

If you're going to confront your boss and you're angry right now, perhaps it would be wiser to wait until your emotions aren't doing your thinking for you.

Confrontation is a lot like removing a splinter from your finger. It is painful for a few minutes, but once you remove the splinter, you feel better. Looking back on it, you realize that taking the splinter out wasn't bad, especially compared with the benefits. This is another example of short-term pain for long-term gain.

Some people fear that confrontation will damage or add distance to a relationship. Here's one way to confront and still keep the other person "near and dear."

D—Describe the situation.

E—Express your feelings.

A—Ask for what you need.

R—Reinforce the other person.

Describe the situation.   In this step you want to be as objective and succinct as possible. This is not the time to list 14 reasons you are upset with someone. Unfortunately, this often is what happens because we fail to confront each other with our small concerns. Instead, we wait until we have collected a laundry list of complaints that we "dump" all at once. This makes you feel better because you got it off your chest. However, it does not resolve the situation because the other person usually feels blamed, attacked, or "dumped on" and is not willing to work toward any changes.

If you do have several concerns, focus on one and let the others wait for another time. This will enable you and the other party to stick to the issue. With one issue rather than several, you reduce the chances that the other party will become defensive. If you can explain how the situation is creating stress for you, the other party will be more able to understand things from your perspective. Remember when we discussed the role of perception in stress (Chapter 1)? The fact that you are experiencing conflict with someone is an indication that each of you perceives the situation in a different way. Once you can stand in each other's shoes, it is much easier to resolve the situation. If you fail to help other people see your point of view, they can only remain locked in their points of view. The goal here is for both persons to expand their points of view and reach a "viewing point."

An analogy will help explain this concept. If you've ever been to the mountains, you know you can stand on the ground, look up, and see a mountain peak. Think of this as your point of view. From this point of view it appears there is only one mountain—the one before you. If you hike up that mountain, though, or take a tram to the top, an amazing thing happens. As you look out from the summit, you suddenly realize there are many more mountains (or points of view), none of which you could see previously. This is what you want to achieve with the other person—the ability of each of you to see the other's point of view.

Express your feelings. After you describe the situation, identify how you are feeling. You might feel upset, frustrated, disappointed, confused, nervous, scared, or anything else. Once you know how you feel, begin your confrontation message with, "I feel _____ (feeling word)." By starting out with *I*, you minimize any chance that the other person will become defensive. Too often, confrontations are begun with the word *you*. Is it any surprise that the other person instantly feels defensive and stops listening?

When you make an *I* statement, you are describing how you feel in the situation, and you are assuming responsibility for those feelings. There is no blame inherent in this statement. When you begin with *you*, an invisible pointing finger seems to accompany your words, and that finger is pointing at the other person, blaming them and holding them responsible for the situation.

Ask for what you need.   After describing the situation and expressing your feelings, make a suggestion about how the situation can be changed. If you don't ask for what you want to be different, how can anyone know what to change? Your co-worker is not being stubborn or resistant; he or she may not have thought of the same solution that you have in mind. If you want to solve the problem with the other person, don't make any assumptions.

Reinforce the other person.   Don't forget to acknowledge the other person! This can be as simple as saying, "Thanks for your consideration," "Thanks for your help," or "I appreciate your cooperation." If the other person actually makes a change, give him or her specific reinforcement for that change. For example, you might say "I notice you aren't smoking during our meetings anymore. Thank you." This reinforcement will help maintain the change you want and make your next confrontation easier.

Let's see how these steps would look in a sample situation. Mike works in the employment services department in a state government agency. He is responsible for compensation and benefits, and during the interview process provides candidates with a salary range for the position they've applied for. Mike feels frustrated and angry because his boss does not use the same salary figures and often hires candidates at above the agreed-upon entry-level salary. Then Mike has to find a way to justify it in the files. He fears that some long-term employees will find out about this practice and file a grievance. Mike now feels stressed and apathetic whenever he meets with candidates because he anticipates that the boss will change whatever salary figures he offers.

After analyzing his situation, Mike decided he wanted to confront his boss about this situation. He felt that if he could get this changed, he would feel good about his job again. This is how he decided to approach the boss.

"Fran, we've had several situations lately in which a candidate tells me you quoted a higher salary than I offered in the initial screening. I feel embarrassed when this happens. And it creates problems for me when I prepare the new employee file and need to justify a starting salary that is above our policy guidelines. This practice makes us vulnerable to a grievance, or even a lawsuit. In the future, would you talk with me before you offer a candidate a higher starting salary, so I can advise you as to whether or not we can support the higher figure if challenged? I appreciate you cooperation."

You can use these same steps when you need to confront someone. You will not want to confront every source of stress. This process requires some thoughtful planning and usually creates some short-term stress of its own. However, if you are experiencing chronic stress with an individual or a situation, then confrontation is an excellent strategy for maintaining a sense of control and managing the stress.

Another strategy that you may find helpful is *feel, felt, found*. This allows you to empathize with another person,

minimize the chances of defensiveness, and construc-
tively present a different point of view. Here's how it
might sound. Kate just sold a customer new carpeting for
her home. The customer has complained that the color is
too dark in the room. Kate tells her customer, "I can understand how you feel. Many people who changed carpet
colors have felt they made a mistake. I've found that over
90 percent were happy with their choice after they gave
themselves a week or so to adjust to it. Please live with it
for a week and I'll check back with you."

If you disagree with someone, it isn't necessary to
become disagreeable. You can disagree in a way that
keeps the focus on the issue and not the person. Here's
how the verbal strategy works:

One thing I like. . . .
My concern is. . . .
An alternative is. . . .

Juan and Jorge disagreed about whether or not to raise the
dues in their professional association. Juan suggested a
$50 increase. Jorge responded like this: "One thing I like
about your suggestion is that we wouldn't need to raise
dues again for at least five years. My concern is that with
the number of members who have been laid off this year,
or had their hours reduced, we will lose members who
need us and whom we need. I'd like to suggest we inves-
tigate fund-raisers as an alternative source of revenue to
raising the dues." Now Juan can respond to Jorge's suggestion without feeling put down or defensive. They can
both focus on the issues.

If you're feeling stress in an interpersonal relationship,
you can use any of the previous three strategies to help
you successfully confront that person. You may find that
the confrontation is stressful; it is for most people. Let me
emphasize again a basic premise of the CALM approach.
You have two choices, short-term pain (confront the

person) for long-term gain (resolve the problem) or short-term gain (say nothing) for long-term pain (suffer with the ongoing stressful behavior). The choice of course is yours. If your choice is not to be responsible for yourself and your own stress level (short-term gain), you are left with two alternatives. You can blame others for the stress you feel or you can play the role of helpless victim. Either way, you'll likely suffer the symptoms of unmanaged stress.

ASK FOR HELP

When you are in a stress-producing situation, it is easy to act the role of the martyr. You expect yourself to be able to do everything and handle everything without help. It's as though asking for help signals that you are incompetent and not able to do the job yourself. This unwillingness to ask or the fear of asking for help is also connected to the wish to have things done "my way." To allow anyone else to assist is to risk that the job won't be done exactly as you would do it. Both these attitudes are outmoded and highly ineffective when it comes to managing stress.

How do you go about asking for help? Anticipate as far in advance as possible situations that may be stressful. Imagine that you have a proposal that should be postmarked on a particular day three weeks from now. This is a complex bid that will require the input of many people. On the day the proposal is due you are scheduled to go out of town. Begin thinking right now about the last-minute tasks that may need to be done, and begin to alert people. In this way, they can leave some gaps in their schedule to accommodate your needs. For example, tell your secretary about the project now, so he or she can take care of routine tasks in advance of the deadline. Notify the

messenger that you will need the proposal hand-deliv-
ered to the post office on that day. Alert other managers
to the potential need for secretarial assistance to prepare
final graphs and charts. Check with the copyroom employees to be certain they can duplicate your proposal
when it becomes necessary. Lining up this kind of support in advance reduces the crisis-management mentality
that is responsible for so much stress. It is also far easier
to ask for help in advance than it is to ask moments before
a deadline.

When you do ask for help, think about who can best
help you. Try to identify several possible resources so that
if one person turns you down you have an alternative.
Specify exactly what you need from them and why. This
allows them to give you honest answers about whether or
not they can help. Understanding the why increases motivation to follow through on the commitment. Tell them
when you will need their help. This way, you can confirm
their availability and they can make necessary arrange-
ments. If you know, also tell them for how long you will
need their help.

With this degree of clarity, there are no surprises on
anyone's part. Too often you are asked to help out, you
agree, and then you find out the task is more complex or
time-consuming than you thought. This leads to resentment and an unwillingness to be a future resource. Be
careful not to abuse your supporters or you may find
yourself working alone!

A simple format you can use is, "Here's my situation
and what I need is. . . ." Once you have expressed your
need, the other person can respond with a yes, a no, or a
compromise.

Asking for and giving help is a two-way street. Don't
expect that others will help you again and again if you
don't return the favor from time to time. In fact, helping

Steps to Ask for Help

1. Put aside the need to be Superhuman and the need to have something done your way.
2. Select the best person to help.
3. Ask for help by explaining your situation, specifying what needs to be done and why, and estimating how long it will take.
4. Get a commitment and let your helpers do what they agreed to do.
5. Express your appreciation.

others whenever you can becomes a good policy because you build what Stephen Covey, in his book *7 Habits of Highly Effective People*, described as emotional bank accounts.[2] During each interaction with another person, you can either make an emotional deposit or an emotional withdrawal. A deposit occurs when you express your appreciation, greet someone, follow through on your commitments, respect a confidence, and so on. These deposits build accounts from which you can make an emotional withdrawal: for example, when you need help with a project, a favor, or maybe understanding on a day when you are short-tempered or out of sorts. If you make more withdrawals than deposits, you can emotionally bankrupt a relationship. That leads to stress!

Managing stress, then, is the art of balance. You balance your capacity with the demands placed on you. You balance your emotional deposits with your emotional withdrawals. You balance yes and no. Ultimately, your goal is to balance your emotional, mental, physical, and spiritual selves.

MANAGE YOUR TIME

After negative thinking (discussed in Chapter 3), the inability to manage time is the second greatest cause of self-imposed stress. Poor time management results in crisis management, which results in stress.

One of the first-time management problems you may run into is not scheduling enough time for a task. Then you'll experience stress because you can't get the task done in the available time. Remember Jerome from the beginning of this chapter? He had a budget to prepare and on the final day found himself running short of time. Part of his problem may have been not allowing enough time to complete the project. This can be tricky because Parkinson was right when he said work expands to fill the time available. So how do you realistically "guesstimate" time needed for projects?

Two techniques work. One is called a Time Log, and the other is called a Project Log. Both will require some time up-front. (Short-term pain for long-term gain again!) Look at this as an investment that will pay big dividends rather than spending or wasting time.

Time Log

A Time Log is a record you keep over a period of one to two weeks, in which you record as accurately as possible what you do during the day. In Figure 2–1, you can see that the day has been broken into 15-minute segments. This is the smallest unit of time most people will need to monitor. You may find it more useful to keep the log in 30- or 60-minute intervals. Make this determination on the basis of how you typically spend your time. For example, if you are a social worker who sees clients every hour, it may be more realistic for you to keep a Time Log with longer time intervals.

FIGURE 2–1
Time Log

	Activity		*Activity*
7:00 A.M.		12:45 P.M.	
7:15 A.M.		1:00 P.M.	
7:30 A.M.		1:15 P.M.	
7:45 A.M.		1:30 P.M.	
8:00 A.M.		1:45 P.M.	
8:15 A.M.		2:00 P.M.	
8:30 A.M.		2:15 P.M.	
8:45 A.M.		2:30 P.M.	
9:00 A.M.		2:45 P.M.	
9:15 A.M.		3:00 P.M.	
9:30 A.M.		3:15 P.M.	
9:45 A.M.		3:30 P.M.	
10:00 A.M.		3:45 P.M.	
10:15 A.M.		4:00 P.M.	
10:30 A.M.		4:15 P.M.	
10:45 A.M.		4:30 P.M.	
11:00 A.M.		4:45 P.M.	
11:15 A.M.		5:00 P.M.	
11:30 A.M.		5:15 P.M.	
11:45 A.M.		5:30 P.M.	
Noon		5:45 P.M.	
12:15 P.M.		6:00 P.M.	
12:30 P.M.		6:15 P.M.	
		6:30 P.M.	

Next develop some codes to represent your most common activities. You will use these codes to save you the time of writing out repetitive and long descriptions when you keep the Time Log. For example, your codes might include:

T   Telephone call
M   Meeting
S   Supervisory conference
R   Reading
I   Interview
RW   Report writing
LW   Letter writing
TR   Travel time
C   Chitchat, socializing
E   Eating, coffee break
B   Brain work, thinking

Add to this list any codes that would represent major activities you perform. You can further refine this by adding numbers to it. Let's say you spend an hour making sales calls. You could record this on your Time Log as T-8, which would tell you it took one hour to make eight calls. The particular system you design for tracking your activities is less important than maintaining an accurate record of what you do with your time.

After you have data from a week or two, you can analyze your Time Log. This is your moment of truth! As you look at your Time Log, you are collecting data on two important aspects of your time. First, where is your time going? Is half of it spent on the phone? How much of your time is being spent in meetings? How much time is lost to coffee breaks and chitchat? (be honest with yourself). How much of your time was spent working on your highest priorities? If you had a major project due, is that where you spent your time, or did your time get eaten up by lower-priority tasks? The more willing you are to be truthful with yourself as you review your Time Log, the more powerful the learning can be. No one else needs to see this; it is for your personal use.

The second stage of analysis is to review your key activities and see just how long they took. If you were preparing your monthly report, how long did it take—1 hour, 15 minutes, 2 hours? How about travel time between appointments—is it taking a couple of hours per week or as much as a couple of days' worth of time? If you were orienting a new employee, how much time was actually spent in that process—was it a couple of hours a *week* or a couple of hours a *day?*

Collecting this information will help you in two ways. First, you will begin to develop a sense of how long a task takes, which will allow you to plan your time more effectively. Let's take the example of a monthly report. Typically you have allowed yourself 30 minutes to put it together before you send it off to be typed. Now, as you review your Time Log, you see that you actually spent one and one-half hours. There wasn't anything unusual about this month's report, and you realize that you have probably been spending about three times as long as you thought on this task. With such concrete data, you can ask yourself how to streamline the process so it only requires 30 minutes. You might also recognize that this task warrants that much time, and in the future you will allow one and one-half hours. If, as you review your Time Log, you see repeatedly that you have estimated less time than a task actually takes, you are identifying what may be one of your major stressors.

Second, you will gain a better understanding of how much flexibility you have in your daily or weekly schedule after you study your Time Log. Most people make one strategic error when they are planning their daily schedules: They plan as if they have eight hours to work with. Most of us do not have 8 hours. That 8-hour day can shrink to 6, 5, or 3 hours depending on your *usual and customary* activities. If your department has a daily update meeting that takes 15 minutes, you have only 7 hours and 45 minutes available to schedule. If you discover from your Time Log that you spend at least 1 hour every day responding to incoming phone calls, you're now down to 6 hours and 45 minutes. Continue studying your Time Log for routine expenditures of time that are part of your job, and subtract them from your working hours. (Note that 30 minutes spent reading the paper, socializing, and drinking coffee every morning is not part of your job. That is wasted time that you need to reclaim.) Once you've done this, you know *realistically* how much time you have available each day to schedule for your high-priority work. If you've been scheduling 8 hours' worth of projects when you really have had only 6 hours and 45 minutes available, you have been creating stress for yourself and probably have been working long hours or taking work home on a regular basis.

The Time Log is such a valuable tool that you will want to use it to check up on yourself at least once a year.

Project Log

The second tool that can be invaluable to you in your planning is a Project Log (Figure 2–2). Large or complex projects may not be completed in the period during which you keep your Time Log. In fact, some projects can take several months to complete. A Project Log allows you to track the various components of a project and the time it takes to complete them. This is valuable for many reasons. If you are in a business such as an accounting or consulting firm, in which you are paid for a particular project, you need to know how long you spend on a project or you

FIGURE 2–2
Project Log

Project: _____

Date Assigned: _____

Estimated Time: _____ Actual Time: _____

Date	Activity	Time (Hours)

may underbid it. Without a Project Log, there is no accurate way at the conclusion of a task to evaluate whether you made money, lost money, or broke even. Even internal projects have a cost-benefit ratio that needs to be assessed.

In one management information system department, Marta submitted a monthly report to senior management. When Marta was on disability leave, Helen prepared the report. Helen decided to track how long it took her to prepare the report and discovered it was five hours. When she submitted the report to her vice president, she attached a note asking if the report was worth the five hours of staff time needed every month to prepare the data. The answer she received was no. Her decision to track her time and provide senior management with that information saved the department five hours every month—that's one and one-half weeks over the course of a year.

You also can benefit from the Project Log for projects that are completed on an annual basis. Fred was responsible for the annual meeting at his company. This involved many tasks, including preparation of the annual report, mailing invitations, selecting guest speakers, arranging for a facility, and ordering meals and decorations. By keeping a careful Project Log, he was able in subsequent years to make a realistic schedule for each of the tasks, reduce his stress, and produce a more successful event.

In successive years, using the Project Log as a basis, you can continue to refine the project, finding ways to save time and even money. When you're promoted and need to delegate this task to a new person, you will have an excellent tool for monitoring progress on the project.

The Time Log and Project Log provide you with benchmarks against which you can plan and measure your progress. It's like an athlete who establishes a baseline performance, then begins the process of looking for ways to be better and faster. Do not try to be *efficient* until you know you are *effective*. In other words, don't try to work faster (efficient) until you know you are doing the right things (effective).

Set Goals

Knowing where you are through the Time Log and Project Log allows you to think about where you want to be. To do this you need goals. If your company does not set goals, you can set them for yourself. Goals are the magic key to prioritizing your time and getting the important things done—effectiveness. Without them, you will likely be very busy (even efficient), but a year from now you'll be in essentially the same place as you are now. A goal works like a magnetic force—it pulls you toward it. The more powerful the goal and the stronger your desire, the greater the pull and the more likely that you will reach it successfully.

You can set a goal for anything: sales, customer service, profits, turnover, growth, new products, and so on. Just be sure your goals are SMART. A SMART goal meets these criteria:

S—Specific
M—Measurable
A—Achievable
R—Realistic
T—Timebound

Specific. What exactly are you going to do? Quantify your goal. It doesn't matter how you quantify, just as long as it is clear and specific.

Measurable. How will you know you have achieved the goal? Remember to have in place whatever recordkeeping procedures you will need. A goal can't be measurable before the measurement devices are in place. If they aren't ready to go, the result is the same as not being able to measure the goal.

For example, your goal may be to reduce customer complaints. However, you don't currently keep track of complaints. How will you know if you achieve your goal if you don't have mechanisms in place to measure it?

Achievable.   Can it be done? Is it possible? Have others done it before you?

Realistic.   Being achievable is not enough. The goal also needs to be realistic. You want it to be a stretch—that will increase your motivation. If it is unrealistic, though, it will become demotivating. Take into consideration what you have done in the past to be more realistic.

Timebound.   Set deadlines for your goals. Without deadlines, you have only dreams, empty words on a piece of paper. Deadlines might coincide with company time cycles such as fiscal year-end, performance appraisal, or calendar year or some other cycle unique to your business. Communicate these deadlines to others so you all are working toward the same deadline. Schedule regular progress checks so you know where you stand against your expected deadlines. This is especially important for long-range goals that may require months or even years to complete.

Don't overwhelm yourself with goals; limit them to three or four. Put the goals in a place where you can see them easily. Then when you are faced with several tasks demanding your attention, look at your goals and ask yourself, Which one of these activities will bring me closer to my goals? That is the one to do.

This kind of strategic time management will result in less stress and more promotions than randomly doing everything that comes across your desk. Think about some of the people who have advanced in your company. They are probably people who have worked successfully on a few key projects, not people who have completed dozens of less valuable projects. If you focus your efforts on activities that move you toward your goals, you can't help but be successful and you will experience less stress in the process.

Consider making your first goal to manage your time more effectively. Choose one of the time wasters you identified while keeping your Time Log and set a goal to decrease or eliminate it. Complete another Time Log in three to six months to check your progress.

Get Organized

- If your manager calls and asks for last week's sales figures and you can't find them, you will feel stress.
- If you fail to put a meeting on your schedule, and while you're writing a report a colleague walks by and says, "Hey, I'll walk to the meeting with you," you're going to feel stress.
- If your secretary gives you a letter to sign and it gets "lost," you have created stress not only for yourself, but also for your secretary.
- If one of your staff members asked for approval on her vacation and you "haven't gotten around to it yet," you have created stress for her.

Do any of these situations sound familiar to you? If the answer is yes, you need to get organized! In the first three situations, you feel stress; in the last two, your lack of organization creates stress not only for yourself, but for others too. You become a stress carrier. Read on for some quick, easy ways to get organized.

Keep a clean desk. If your desk isn't clear of all papers except the ones you're working on, you can't be as organized as you can when the desk is clear. Take the time to go through what is on it today and either file or throw away all that paper. Set up baskets for incoming work and outgoing work. Create a file for things you need to read. Develop a coding system to separate those items that need immediate attention, such as correspondence, from those that can wait.

Keep a daily schedule. Carry it with you so that if a meeting or appointment is scheduled, you can record it immediately. Use it to jot down notes to yourself about things you need to remember. For example, if you have a meeting scheduled, you might make a note to yourself to bring a copy of the last meeting's minutes. If you are meeting with someone outside the company, you might write down his or her phone number.

Keep frequently used information handy. If you are working on four projects, keep those files easily accessible so you don't need to shuffle through your filing cabinet for them. Make a list of frequently used phone numbers and keep it near the phone. Get a wall chart for scheduling multiple projects, so you can glance up and see what needs to be done and where you are against the deadline. Keep important customer information in a readily accessible form, whether on address cards or a printout. If you routinely find yourself looking up information, you probably need to maintain it in some more accessible form.

Use a *To Do* list. Every day make a list of things that need to be done. Then prioritize them against your goals. If something new comes up during the day, look at your list and ask yourself which task is more important.

Manage Your Time
1. Periodically keep a Time Log.
2. Routinely maintain a Project Log.
3. Develop SMART goals.
4. Get organized! Keep your desk clean, maintain a daily schedule, keep frequently used information handy, and use a *To Do* list.

Once you have made your list, start with the most important things first. Try to give yourself a time guesstimate for the task and then stick with it. You can do more with a time frame than without it. This is essential when you are managing multiple priorities. If you don't schedule some time each day or week for every project, you may find yourself unable to meet deadlines.

Once you begin to manage your time more effectively, your stress will decrease. These ideas and techniques can help you change the situation you are in to give you more control, and thereby less stress.

LEARN TO SAY NO

Peter Senge in his book *The Fifth Discipline* emphasized the importance of using a systems perspective to understand the behavior of individuals and organizations.[3] Certain behaviors are the natural consequence of systems that are in place. Of relevance here is his discussion on how difficult it is to balance the demands of home and work. People have the best intentions of balancing them, yet something happens and their life becomes unbalanced.

Here's how Senge describes the systemic nature of the problem.

If you spend lots of time working, you will probably receive positive feedback from your peers and boss. This reinforces your working and makes you want to work more to get even more positive feedback. Meanwhile, the members of your family likely feel excluded from your life because you spend so much time working. They may also feel disappointed that you've missed some family times, like a child's soccer game or a birthday, in order to work. Consequently, being at home may feel unpleasant because of your guilt and family members' complaints about your absences. Being at home causes negative feedback. If you think of it systemically, it makes sense that you would increase your time at work where you get positive reinforcement, and decrease time with your family where you get negative reinforcement.

The system could also work in reverse. In other words, you could spend time attending all your kids' sporting events, volunteering with the school and for other community activities. You are rewarded with the affection of your family and community service awards by your community. The more you get involved, the more you are asked to participate in special community projects. At work, when you are asked to take on a special assignment that will require overtime, or out-of-town travel, you decline. After the second or third time this happens, people at work begin to describe you as "uncommitted," "just working for a paycheck," or "not a team player." Therefore, when the next special assignment comes up, you aren't asked. You begin to feel left out of the camaraderie that others have developed working together on projects. Your family and community life takes on increasing importance because that is where you are rewarded. Your work life seems less important because there are negative feelings associated with it. The system is in place the same as the previous example, just in the opposite direction.

To manage your stress and achieve the balance you want in your life demands that you know what your values are. Then you need to set personal priorities in alignment with those values. It means you need to know when and how to set limits. If you want to balance work and home, you will need to consciously decide when to say yes and when to say no. If these aren't conscious decisions, the system will play itself out and you'll lose that precious thing called *balance*. But you need to know *how* to say no.

Many people have trouble saying no because they operate under the Myth of Obligation. You may too if you believe that if someone makes a request of you, you are obligated to say yes. Therefore, you don't feel you have the right to say no. If you do say no, you suffer from feelings of guilt.

You forget that if a person asks a question, they are prepared for a yes or a no. If they want only a yes, they will make a statement, not a request.

There are five steps you can follow when refusing a request.

1. Pay attention to how you feel when the request is made. Often you will notice a sinking feeling in your stomach because you do not want to do something. This is an early warning signal that you need to refuse the request.

2. Ask questions. How often have you agreed to something and later, when you found out what you agreed to, regretted your decision? Before you agree to something, make sure you know what you are agreeing to do. Don't forget to ask yourself the questions listed on page 44.

3. After you have collected information about both your feelings and the content of the request, decide. Don't be rushed! If you need to think it over, do so. If someone pressures you for a decision before you have time to consider it, refuse. If your decision is to decline, say no. That two-letter word can be very powerful. Less specific

phrases, such as "I'm not sure," or "Let me think about it," usually turn into yes.

4. Avoid excuses and explain only when it's appropriate. People use excuses when they want to say no, thinking they will soften the refusal. Often an excuse turns into a yes because the other party comes back with a solution to your problem (excuse). Rather than use an excuse, if you have an explanation, give it. An explanation says you would if you could, but you can't. It is not necessary to go into great detail with an explanation. For example, imagine you are asked to work late for the third time this week. You want to be with your family, and you need a break from the work. You could give an excuse: for example, "I promised my partner I'd take care of the kids." Then your boss can come back, "Why don't you get a sitter?" or "Bring them into the office. They can watch a video while you work." Now you're stuck. You'll probably say yes when you wanted to say no. Rather than make an excuse, explain by saying something like, "I have another commitment tonight." This is honest, yet precludes a long, drawn-out explanation. If the circumstance warrants it, you can give the full explanation. In this case, it might be "I made a commitment to my family that I wouldn't be away from home more than three nights a week. I've already worked two nights, and I serve on a committee at church, which commits a third night. I want to honor the commitment I made to my family. I won't be able to work late tonight."

5. Stick to your original explanation, even if the other person persists in the request. This is known as the *broken-record technique*. You do this calmly and without getting upset. In the situation described above, if your boss said, "What kind of commitment?" you would respond, "I regret I can't work late tonight. I have a previous commitment." Most people will not press you after you use the broken-record technique if you do it without getting angry or defensive.

How to Say No
1. How do you feel about the request? Do you want to do it?
2. Ask questions. Be sure you know what you're being asked to do.
3. Say no if that's your decision.
4. Explain; don't use an excuse.
5. Use the broken-record technique, if necessary.

TAKE A BREAK

Sometimes the simplest way to manage stress is to get away from the situation for a little while. That "little while" may be five minutes, or it may be a two-week vacation.

More research into the functioning of the brain is being done all the time. We now understand that there are two hemispheres, the left and right, which perform different tasks. The left hemisphere is responsible for language and rational and linear thinking. It likes numbers and order. The right hemisphere is the creative, problem-solving side. It operates more intuitively and sees wholes rather than parts. You need both sides. However, you may rely heavily on the left side in your work and spend many hours concentrating on a task or problem. Research shows that the left brain needs little "stretch breaks" about every hour. You will actually be more productive if you stop and shift hemispheres than if you try to push yourself as if you were running an endurance race.

What does this mean for you? Every hour you need to rest your left brain for a few minutes. Stop and take a few deep breaths. Spend a few minutes looking out your window, if you have one. Get up and walk to the drinking fountain. Let your brain relax for a moment. Please note that this not a suggestion to take a 15-minute coffee break, go smoke a cigarette, or gossip with others in the office. It is a brief shift of focus for your brain and body.

If you doubt the power of these minibreaks, think of a time when you were trying to solve a problem, but try as you might, you could not come up with an answer. Then, while you were driving home, taking a walk, or taking a shower, the answer came to you as an "Aha" out of the blue. The answer came when you turned the problem over to your right brain. You can facilitate those Ahas by giving yourself brief time-outs on a regular basis.

You also need longer breaks from your work, in the form of weekends and vacations. These are opportunities for you to renew yourself. Many people have felt ready to quit a job, but after a week or two away returned refreshed, relaxed, and highly productive.

When you work for extended periods of time without breaks, you begin to lose perspective. Disagreements and disappointments get out of proportion. You may take trivial matters too seriously. As you learned in Chapter 1, this is an early warning sign of burnout.

If you've been priding yourself on how hard you work and how long it has been since you took a vacation, you are courting burnout. Another surprise—you may not be as effective as you think you are.

When you do take a break, make sure it is just that— no work while you're on vacation! No calling the office every day or having the office call you. No one is indispensable. To pretend that you are is destructive to yourself and to the others around you. A stress-management challenge is to leave your work at the office. So much of today's work is mental that it is possible to lay on a beach and still be working. That doesn't count as a break. The kind of break being discussed here is a mental break. You need to be able to separate from your work mentally and

---

Take a Break
1. Give yourself minivacations about once an hour.
2. Use your vacation time!
3. When you're extra busy, shorten breaks—don't eliminate them.

---

put 100 percent of your attention elsewhere. The more you are able to find activities you can lose yourself in, the more refreshed you will feel when you return to your work. This simple axiom—be present to what you are doing—will go a long way toward reducing your stress.

Breaks will help you maintain balance, which is critical for managing stress. The harder you're working, the greater the demands, the more pressing the deadlines, the more you need to stop and breathe and to take a break.

ANTICIPATE STRESSORS AND PREPARE FOR THEM

You can anticipate many of the stressors you experience, such as preparing an annual budget, quarterly reports, or performance appraisals. When you know a stressor is upcoming, you can make some plans in advance to reduce its impact. Use all the suggestions in the preceding sections. In addition, here are other ways you can prepare for an anticipated stressor:

1. Don't take on any new projects that will demand a lot of your time or come due during the time of the expected stressor.

2. Take care of as much routine work in advance of the stressful time as possible.

3. Alert others about your stressful time, and advise them you will not be able to take on additional projects during that time.

4. Build in a reward for yourself (for example, take a vacation as soon as the project is complete).

5. Tell you family and friends about the stressful time and ask for their support and understanding.

6. During the stressful time, schedule some getaways for yourself to help you keep your perspective. These might include a weekend away, a regular night out, or any activity engaging enough to help you set work aside for a few hours.

7. Eat nutritious foods and get some exercise.

8. Be ruthless with your time. Do not take on any commitments that will increase your stress level. Say no graciously and regularly. Know your goals and priorities and keep them uppermost in your mind.

SUMMARY

The first step to help you CALM down is to change the situation when you can. Start by giving yourself some time to take a deep breath and think for a few moments before you plunge into coping with the situation. Ask yourself the seven empowering questions that will put you in control of the situation:

Can someone else do it?

Can it be delayed?

Can something else be substituted?

Is it essential?

Will a job aid help?

Can the stress be avoided?

Can the stressor be confronted?

If you answer yes to any of these questions, use the following skills to make changes: confront the situation, ask for help, manage your time, say no, take a break, and prepare for expected stressors.

The purpose of managing stress is to maintain long-term health and well-being. To achieve that may require short-term stress in terms of taking action to change the situation. Clear values will help you make the difficult choices that lead to wellness instead of burnout.

In the next chapter, you'll learn what you can do if you can't change the situation.

Chapter Three

The A of CALM: Accept What Can't Be Changed

Thomas Crum, in his book *The Magic of Conflict*, recounts this well-known story of a samurai.

> In the orient, there is a story of a samurai who is being chased by a bear. He literally runs off a cliff. As he's falling, he grabs a branch.
>
> He looks up and sees the bear leaning over the cliff, clawing at his head, missing only by inches. As he looks down to the ground below, only about 15 feet, he sees a lion leaping up, missing his feet by only inches. As he looks at the branch he is clutching, he sees two groundhogs gnawing away at it. He watches as his lifeline disappears, bite by bite.
>
> As he takes a deep, long breath, he notices, next to his branch, a clump of wild strawberries. In the midst of the clump is a great, red, juicy strawberry. With his free hand, he reaches over, picks the strawberry, puts it in his mouth, chews it slowly, and says, "Ah—delicious."[1]

There are situations that you cannot control and cannot change despite your best efforts. Some examples include a merger or buyout, a boss with personal problems, certain deadlines, new management, new government regulations, foreign competition, the weather, and other people's behavior. If you persist in trying to control these situations, you only create more stress for yourself. What can you do so you are not powerless in these situations? You can learn to act like the samurai.

In other words, breathe, stay calm and present, and accept the situation for what it is. Acceptance is not the same thing as giving up. Acceptance is a *choice* you make that puts you back in control. When you accept a situation, you participate in an active process, not a passive one. You make a conscious decision to move past judgment, or past being angry and upset, to face the reality before you. This requires maturity. Most people find it easier to gripe and complain about a situation than to face it squarely and accept it for what it is.

If you have a completely unreasonable boss, and all efforts to improve communication or remove yourself from the situation have been unsuccessful (the first step of the model, change the situation), you are faced with how to manage the stress. You could participate with colleagues in telling "ain't it awful" stories or you could complain to family and friends. These coping behaviors momentarily let off steam, but you remain upset about the situation. Following the model, the best way to manage this situation is to accept that you are working for a difficult boss, and there will be tensions between the two of you. Paradoxically, such acceptance is powerful; you gain a sense of control when you see things as they are. When you stop resisting the truth, you aren't as rigid psychologically or physically. As you alter yourself and your perceptions, you just might discover that others begin to change! There's a paradox at work here: To change others, alter yourself. Wishing and complaining don't change reality; they do add to the stress you feel.

This is not to say you can't express dissatisfaction or disappointment with a situation. You can, and that can be healthy. Once it is expressed, however, move on. Expressing it over and over becomes complaining. Remember Fred, who was planning the annual meeting in

Chapter 2? He wanted an overhead projector for the meeting. When one wasn't available, he had several choices. He could complain to everyone he met that the meeting facility didn't follow through and that now the meeting wouldn't be as effective as he planned, or he could accept the reality of the situation and decide how he was going to respond to it. The second choice would reduce Fred's stress and the stress of those around him. He doesn't have to get stuck in feelings of disappointment.

CHANGE YOUR THINKING

You will find acceptance much easier if you are willing to change your perceptions and attitudes about a situation. You create more stress internally with your thoughts than is ever caused by external events. As Epictetus said in the first century A.D., "Men are disturbed not by things, but by the views which they take of them."

Fred might say to himself, "This is awful! This could cost me my job! The president will be furious when he finds out there isn't an overhead projector. I knew I should have brought the projector myself!" When he reacts this way, he creates self-imposed stress. His thoughts give him more of a problem than the missing projector.

Dr. Albert Ellis, author of *A New Guide to Rational Living*, developed a model for understanding how thoughts about a situation create feelings and behavior. In his model, situations are neutral—neither positive nor negative. However, you form beliefs about situations and these beliefs create feelings that lead to behaviors. If Fred's beliefs and thoughts are negative, they will cause him to feel frustrated, angry, and upset. That will result in some form of external behavior such as yelling at others, muscle tension, or self-criticism.

Science, through the use of positron-emission tomography, has taken Ellis's theory one step further. Thoughts can literally change the shape of the body. If one cell is happy, all cells are happy. If one cell is sad, all cells are sad.[2] People know this intuitively and use the expressions, "He's aged 10 years since his wife died," or "She looks 10 years younger since she moved to Florida."

Applying Ellis's theory to Fred's situation, imagine how differently he might behave if he thought, "Mistakes happen. This is certainly not the end of the world. I will alert the president and together perhaps we can come up with an alternative." This kind of self-talk will make Fred feel in control, confident, and relaxed. He will approach the president in this frame of mind and be more likely to reach a satisfactory outcome.

Aside from the stress caused by physical stressors in the environment (for example, noise, air pollution, and furniture), all other stress is a result of perception or thoughts. To be able to accept reality for what it is without distorting it by criticizing, judging, or having other negative thoughts is a very powerful stress-management technique.

Check your thoughts against the following list of negative thoughts.[3] The more of these you recognize in yourself, the greater the likelihood that you are creating stress for yourself. Put a check mark in front of any of the thought patterns you use.

_____ **Overgeneralization.**   There are two words that signal you are overgeneralizing: *always* and *never*. These words distort reality because situations neither *always* occur nor *never* occur. Both words lead to feelings of victimization, the opposite of the in-control feeling you need in order to manage stress. Let's look at an example.

Betsy is preparing to leave for a long-awaited two-week vacation. At about 2:00 P.M., her boss comes in with an urgent project and says, "It has to be done before you leave." Betsy grudgingly takes the project, and as she starts to look through it thinks to herself, "I always get these last-minute projects dumped on me. They never let you leave this place without trying to get one more thing out of you!"

How do you imagine Betsy is feeling? How is she likely to interact with her boss the rest of the afternoon? Just by her thoughts she has created stress and will probably respond irritably to her boss and colleagues the rest of the afternoon. In addition, having activated the stress response, she is likely to have more difficulty concentrating on the task, which will further add to her stress.

To interrupt this negative pattern, Betsy needs to change her thinking. She would not compound her stress if she thought something like, "I will look at this and do the best I can in the time I have left."

When you catch yourself saying *always* or *never* to yourself, stop and change your self-talk. Eliminate those words and replace them with only the facts. Practice describing reality as accurately as you can without any judgment or overgeneralizing. Think through how you could change the following examples of overgeneralization to more positive self-talk.

1. I'm always the last one to know.
2. I'll never get this finished.
3. She'll never hire me.

Here are some possible alternatives.

1. Purchasing knew the name of the new vice president before accounting did.
I just learned that we're out of stock on that item.

2. I have one more wall to paint before I can go home.
   This project is taking longer than I anticipated.
3. I didn't handle the interview questions as well as I wanted to.
   I don't have a college degree.

_____ **All-or-nothing thinking.** In this form of negative thinking, you see things as extremes—either perfect and wonderful or imperfect and awful. There are no shades of gray. Of course this is not the way reality is. To make a mistake is not the same thing as being a failure. To experience a disappointment is not the same thing as being unsuccessful. Not finishing a project is not the same as not starting it. To be less than perfect does not warrant criticism. See if you can identify the all-or-nothing thinking in the following situation.

John did not receive the promotion he applied for. This was the second time he had been passed over. While having lunch with one of his friends that day, he said, "Well, Steve, I've just about decided to change professions. It's pretty obvious that I'm not cut out to be an engineer. After all, I've been passed over twice now. I'll never get anywhere as an engineer. I'm just no good at it."

Because John is passed over for a promotion does not mean he is not cut out to be an engineer, nor does it mean he will never get anywhere. Did you catch the overgeneralization in that last phrase? John is adding to his disappointment by criticizing himself needlessly and viewing a disappointment as an indication that he cannot be successful.

He would lessen his stress while still acknowledging the disappointment if he said something different to himself and his friend. A more CALMing response might be, "I feel disappointed about not getting the promotion. This is the second time I've been passed over. I need to find out if I am missing a necessary skill, if my interview skills are weak, if I lack some experience, or just where the problem lies. I still want that kind of position, and I'm willing to learn what I need to do to get that job in the future."

Notice that the second response is more descriptive and less judgmental. He keeps it positive by staying in the present with how he feels right now and by reaffirming what he wants. He is not looking back with recriminations, nor is he looking forward with "what ifs." To learn to stay in the here and now, or present to the moment, is a great stress reducer. The past and the future exist only in the mind. The present is current reality. Stress occurs when you leave present reality and worry about the past or future.

Do you recognize yourself as a person who falls into the trap of all-or-nothing thinking? The solution, as with overgeneralization, is to describe your situation as accurately as you can. Describe your feelings as just that—feelings. Be careful about turning your feelings into explanations or justifications for what is. In the second response John said, "I feel disappointed." In the first response he didn't identify his feelings, but instead translated them into "I'm not cut out to be an engineer."

_____ **Mental filter.** When you mental filter, your mind focuses on one aspect of a situation (usually negative) to the exclusion of anything else in the situation. It's almost as if that one part of the situation is magnetized, and it draws your undivided attention. Take the situation of Sunita, for example.

It was with excitement that Sunita opened the box with the new training catalog. This project had been nearly a year in the making. Then she saw it: the cover was not printed on the enamel paper stock she had ordered! As she flipped through the pages, she couldn't get her mind off of the cover. A colleague came over and picked up one of the catalogs. As he went through it, he complimented Sunita on the design, layout, use of pictures, and detailed descriptions. For every positive remark he offered, Sunita countered with, "Yeah, but did you see how dull the cover is?" Sunita's mental filtering didn't allow her to notice any of the positive parts of her project. Even if someone else mentions them, she returns her focus to the one thing that is wrong. She's magnetized to what's wrong instead of what's right. Reality is that things go wrong and don't meet your expectations. To be unwilling to accept this is to mentally create stress for yourself. Sunita has lost her perspective by focusing on only one aspect of the situation.

Sunita would be more effective if she handled the situation differently. Instead of focusing only on what she didn't like, Sunita could identify all the parts that pleased her as well as the parts that didn't. This a more realistic assessment. Then Sunita could decide if she wants to take any action to solve the problem of the covers. The covers may be less significant when Sunita is able to see the total picture. As long as she is using a mental filter, she is locked into the powerless position of being unable to take any action to change things. As soon as she changes her thinking, she can move into a problem-solving mode.

_____ **Should, ought, must, have to.** Most people use these words as a regular part of their vocabularies. That is unfortunate because these few words are responsible for many negative feelings and much low self-esteem. Each of these words represents not what you want to do or what you need to do, but what *someone else* wants you to do. They are relics of your past conditioning.

Most *shoulds, oughts, musts,* and *have-to's* come from your early childhood years. They may reflect the wishes of your parents, your teachers, your religious instructors, or any other authority figures. *Should, ought, must* and *have to* are value judgments. When you are young, you don't have the capability as adults do of reasoning. You do not discriminate what information you take in; you just absorb it all. Then in adult life you find that some of what you internalized works for you, and some does not. However, you have not learned to "throw away" the messages that do not apply to you. Instead you carry them around in the form of *shoulds.* When you encounter situations that trigger one of those childhood messages, you apply *should* to yourself and feel guilty and often stressed. In the example below, you will see how Tony uses this form of negative thinking to create stress for himself. He too was passed over for a promotion.

"I knew I should have worn the other suit. I just don't think they took me seriously enough. And when they asked me that question about my relationship with my boss, I never should have said there are times we disagree. I ought to know they don't want any troublemakers, and they probably thought I would be one from my answer. Why do I always have to say the wrong things in interviews? After as many interviews as I've had, I should handle them better by now."

How would *you* be feeling if you had just said this to yourself? Pretty inadequate, don't you think? Tony holds an underlying belief that he *should* be perfect. When reality shows he is not, he berates himself with *shoulds.* In this way *shoulds* can be damaging to your self-esteem.

We also liberally apply *shoulds* to other people and their behavior. Whenever we do this, we are being judgmental, and other people feel it. This is why you sometimes get a defensive reaction from others for no apparent reason.

You have probably told them something they *should* or *shouldn't* do. As you go through this book, you will discover that aside from this section and some examples there are no *shoulds, oughts, musts,* or *have-to's.* Most self-help books are filled with these judgmental phrases. By the time you reach the end, you feel guilty about all the things you aren't doing right or aren't doing at all.

In contrast, throughout this book you will be asked to *consider* ideas. At times you will be told gently of an action or behavior you *need* in order to reach your goals. At other times you will be advised of actions you will *want* to try for desired outcomes. These are the magic words—*choose, prefer, consider, need, want*—that you can start using to replace your *shoulds, oughts, musts,* and *have-to's.* You will be astounded at the difference it makes in how you feel about yourself, and you will be equally impressed with the different responses you get from others.

Tony can change his self-talk as follows.

"At the next interview I'll wear a different suit. I believe I lost some of my credibility when I chose this one. I also want to handle the interview questions differently. It is probably wise to consider in advance how I will respond to the questions about my relationship with my boss. This time I wasn't prepared for the question and I didn't come across the way I wanted to."

Now, wouldn't you feel differently about yourself after this kind of talk than after the other? If this was the only change you decided to make after reading this book, it would be a significant one.

_____ **Disqualifying the positive.** In this form of negative thinking you refuse to accept any positive feedback about yourself or your performance. If you receive a compliment, you find some way to turn it back to the sender or reduce its impact. It's a subtle form of discounting yourself and also, surprisingly enough, the person who gives you the positive feedback. Used on a regular basis it is powerful enough to actually train others not to give you any compliments.

Watch how Molly responds in the next example when a colleague tells her what a great job she did getting the figures prepared for a marketing analysis: "Oh, it was nothing, really. I just looked through some old reports and summarized their findings. Anybody could have done it if they had taken the time."

Can you see how Molly has discounted the feedback she received? Inadvertently she is telling her colleague, "What makes you think this was such a big deal? Aren't you exaggerating just a little?" Molly's response will put her colleague in the awkward position of trying to "convince" Molly to accept the compliment, or her colleague can withdraw the compliment. Either way, if this happens many times, the colleague will decide it isn't worth the effort to give Molly any praise.

Molly could handle this situation better simply by saying, "Thank you." If she chose to, she could elaborate further and add, "It did take several hours to put together and I appreciate your noticing." This is also an opportunity for Molly to seek further information about her performance. If she is told she did a "great job," she can ask a clarifying question such as "What specifically did you like about it?" This gives her more information on how she can replicate this desirable performance in the future. These responses all build Molly's self-esteem rather than eroding it. As you will learn in Chapter 5, self-esteem is one of the keys for managing stress. Being suspicious of the compliment or disqualifying it adds to Molly's stress.

Many people were taught to be modest and to them this means denying their strengths and refusing compliments. If this is true for you, learning to accept a compliment will be a new behavior that will take some practice.

_____ **Jumping to conclusions.** With this thought pattern you make up an outcome to a situation. It may have some basis in fact, but your conclusion is usually an assumption. Then you behave as if the often-faulty assumption is the truth. Let's look at an example. Don recently opened a new branch office. The sales figures so far are lower than he projected. This is what goes through his mind as he reviews the first quarter's figures.

"These figures are way below projections. I made the wrong decision to open this office. People in Corporate are probably going to want my resignation. Now I know why the VP hasn't returned my phone calls. He probably doesn't want to talk to me until after I get my notice from personnel."

Don may have made an unwise decision; we all do so from time to time. Corporate may, in fact, want to discuss this with him. However, he is creating stress for himself before the fact by jumping to the conclusion that he will be asked to submit his resignation and that this is the reason his phone calls have not been returned. If Don had been told when he opened the new branch that failure to meet projections would result in dismissal, that's one thing. We can't assume that, though, from our example. As for the phone calls not being returned, we all know that is a too-common occurrence in business.

Don would be wiser to face reality clearly—he hasn't met projections—and to design a strategy for how to respond to this. Perhaps he will want to be proactive and call a meeting himself with senior management to discuss the shortfall. Maybe he will design a new tactic for getting the business he needs for the coming quarter. Either of these strategies puts him back in charge of the situation rather than feeling helpless and at the mercy of someone else.

Jumping to conclusions can also affect your future interactions with people. Don might begin to distance himself from senior management in anticipation of termination. If anyone offers suggestions, he may respond defensively or not at all, being convinced it won't matter anyway. His thoughts and beliefs create his own reality and his own destiny. For better or worse you get what you expect.

_____ **Fortune-telling.** This resembles jumping to conclusions. When you are fortune-telling, it's as if you look into a crystal ball and predict the future. Most people enjoy doing this from time to time, and there isn't anything wrong with doing it as long as you don't take it one more step and act as if that prediction is a truth. Using Don's situation again let's go back a little further in time to when he was considering opening a branch office. He has collected all the data in support of the new office and is reviewing them in his office. As he goes through the figures, he thinks to himself, "Nah, Corporate will never go for this idea. They want sure-fire projects. I can't see them being willing to take a risk on this project. The numbers do look good, but I'm not setting myself up to be embarrassed when they turn the idea down."

Don never submits his idea. He and the company lose because while he's sitting there fortune-telling management's negative response, a competitor opens an office in the same location Don would have proposed. How many wonderful opportunities have been lost by American businesses because a creative employee engaged in fortune-telling and never took the risk of presenting his or her ideas? How many times have you not applied for a promotion, expected the worst from a new boss, or refused to make a decision because of fortune-telling? Replace your crystal ball with reality, and not only will you be more effective, you won't suffer from *imaginary* stress.

Fortune-telling is different from planning. Both look to the future. In fortune-telling you predict an outcome and behave as if it's already true. In planning, you create an outcome you want in your mind or on paper and then go about the work of bringing your plan into reality.

The key difference between fortune-telling and jumping to conclusions is that fortune-telling is a mental exercise. In contrast, jumping to conclusions is based on reality. You observe some behavior; then you go about the mental work of interpreting it. In both cases, once the mental work has begun, it isn't checked against reality for change or correction.

_____ **Labeling.**   Do you remember being taught as a child that "if you can't say something nice, don't say anything at all"? You need to recall that phrase when you are working with someone who doesn't meet your expectations or standards. You also need to be gentler with yourself, particularly when you make errors. It is not necessary to attack and criticize yourself or call yourself names. That behavior only makes you feel bad inside, upsets you, and leads to increased stress. Even if you don't use labeling yourself, you've likely heard many of the following expressions used by others around the office:

"What a jerk!"

"I can't believe I'm so dumb."

"You can't talk sense to a crazy man."

"Only an idiot could do what I just did!"

And other, more colorful expressions!

Each of these statements leads to emotional upset. You certainly don't want to believe you're dumb, a jerk, or an idiot. It is also extremely stressful to work with, for, or around someone who is like that. These labels, like the other negative thoughts, distort reality. People cannot be described with a single label, positive or negative. People change depending on the situations in which they find themselves. Remember, from one person's point of view, his or her behavior makes perfect sense. You will reduce your stress by seeking to understand that point of view and reaching for a viewing point instead of using labels and thereby being judgmental.

As long as you judge others, you will judge yourself. Judgment is a source of stress and causes low self-esteem. It's the opposite of acceptance.

_____ **Catastrophizing.** If you "make a mountain out of a molehill," you are catastrophizing. Put another way, it is like taking a snapshot of a problem, then having it blown up into a wall-size poster. In the process, the picture becomes distorted and you don't see the situation as it really is. Don was catastrophizing as well as jumping to conclusions in our earlier example. Not meeting projections for one quarter is hardly enough information on which to base a "go or no-go" decision (although in today's short-term culture it often seems that way). Often catastrophizing is accompanied by *what ifs*, each worse than the one preceding it, so that in just a few minutes you have gone from point A to point Z. Watch how this happens in the following example. Jean has just been told that one of her key staff members has resigned to take a position with a competitor. That afternoon Jean schedules an appointment with her boss to discuss the resignation. This is what she says.

"This is terrible! I don't know how we'll get along without Debbie. She has more experience around here than anyone else. And where will I ever find someone with her skills and her ability to get along with others? You know she was the buffer in our department between Marsha and Doug. Now they will be fighting again. Plus, Debbie knew all our pricing strategies, which the competition will now have. She had such good relationships with her customers that they'll probably all move to the new company with her. We'd better prepare ourselves for a bad quarter. This is going to be awful!"

Does this sound exaggerated? Debbie may be a big loss to the company, but Jean has lost touch with reality and crossed over to catastrophizing. In the process she is upsetting herself and failing to do what she needs to do, which is to begin to plan for how she will replace Debbie and to cover her assignments in the interim. Jean's thinking, not the situation, is the cause of this unnecessary stress. So far she hasn't used any of her energy to reduce her stress or solve the problems she faces.

A better response when she meets with her boss might be, "Debbie has been a key employee here for years. She resigned today and that will have a serious impact on our customers and our department. Because she is going to a competitor, I think it is important that we quickly hire a replacement who can initiate contact with her customers. If we don't act soon, I'm concerned some of them may follow her to her new employer. Will you authorize personnel to begin an immediate search?"

There's quite a difference between the two ways of responding to the situation, isn't there? Are you beginning to see that no matter how difficult or challenging reality might be, it is consistently easier to respond to *it* than to the situations we create with our thoughts? The second step of the CALM approach is to face reality and accept it. Don't embellish it. To do so will only create stress. You will discover that as you accept situations for what they are, you will also accept yourself. It will be easier to flow. You won't find yourself as tense and tight from resisting. You just might find that what used to create distress can now create eustress.

Look back over the list of negative thoughts. How many check marks do you have? Are you willing to change any of these patterns? This is a good time to make a commitment to yourself to start accepting what you cannot change instead of making it worse with your thoughts. You can monitor your own progress by noticing when you start to feel stressed. Then check in with your self-talk. Is it positive or negative? If it's negative, the first change you might want to make to the situation is your internal state of being.

DON'T WORRY

Sometimes you leave the present and drift into another time zone. You float into the past, where you rehash what you did, what you decided, and what you said. You also may drift into the future and agonize about what might happen and what might not happen—what ifs. Neither of these behaviors is productive. Each is a form of worry that produces self-imposed stress. Yet nearly everyone worries from time to time. What can you do if you're a worrier? There are several techniques you can use.

The first is to bring your worry into alignment with reality. Eighty percent of what you worry about never happens. Ten percent of what you worry about is going to happen, and there is not a thing you can do about it besides cope when it does. The last 10 percent is made up of things whose impact you can reduce by taking action.

Take a moment right now and write down some of your worries. The list is already started for you with common worries identified by other businesspeople.

1. What will happen to the economy?
2. Will I get the raise I want?
3. What does the boss think of me?
4. Do my colleagues like me?
5. Will I be laid off?
6. _____

7. _____

8. _____

Now, looking at your list of worries, ask yourself the following questions.

What is the worst that could happen? Think about what it is that you fear. Don't catastrophize, but look honestly at reality and identify the worst possible outcomes. Imagine that a manager is worried about which candidate to hire for a new staff position. What is the worst that could happen? He might make the wrong decision and need to go through the same process again in a few months. Give yourself enough time to think through all your fears.

How likely is it that the worst will happen? Keeping your worst fear in mind, assign a percentage to the probability it will occur. If you think it's not very likely, ask yourself what that means: 20 percent, 10 percent, 5 percent? Be as specific as you can. Our manager might decide there is a 10 percent chance this candidate won't work out and he will need to start the process over. Already he is beginning to put this concern into perspective. Once you do this, you can often leave the worry behind.

Could you live with it if the worst happened? Notice you are asking if you could live with it, not would you like it. If your worst-case scenario did happen, it would undoubtedly be difficult to cope with, but could you live with it? Our manager, if honest, will say yes, he could live with it. Firing the first candidate, beginning the search process anew, and then training another person may not be how he would like to spend his time and energy; however, he could do it. With this question, you are testing your personal strengths and resources. You're asking yourself if you could come to accept this worst situation. It is extremely rare for people to answer no to this question when they are totally honest.

If the worst does happen, how will you cope? This question helps you project yourself into the future. This is the planning, or rehearsal, stage. What would you do? As you are able to picture yourself handling the situation, you build confidence and regain control. Difficult though it might be, you can already visualize what you might do. Our manager knows exactly what the qualifications are for the job; he would pull out the old advertisements and reuse them in the paper. Before he placed an ad, though, he would recontact his second choice candidate and see if he is still available. He might not even need to advertise again!

This step actually allows you to be more proactive today. By anticipating the worst and beginning to plan for it, you can build into your activities right now things that will make coping with your worst-case scenario easier if you are ever faced with it.

After this mental exercise, many people find their worries shrink to a manageable size. They regain control instead of feeling at the mercy of their worry.

Will the intellectual analysis work in all cases? No, sometimes you need another technique called *thought stopping*. This technique works just the way it sounds— you stop the obsessive worry thought. You do this by noticing your thought process. You become an observer of your own mind. As soon as you start to worry, tell yourself, Stop! Your purpose is to interrupt the worry thought.[4]

Picture the child's game of musical chairs. The music is playing and the children are walking in a circle around a row of chairs. Suddenly the music stops and one of the chairs is pulled away. Someone is out of the game. Worry sends you running around in circles like the music does. When you stop the thought—that is, turn off the music— you can pull the chair out from under worry. The game is over.

Once you interrupt the worry thought, you will need to replace it with something else—another thought that is positive and soothing. Try replacing worry with its opposite. If you're worried about choosing the wrong job applicant, replace that thought with, I make wise decisions. Such positive thoughts are called *affirmations*. You will learn more about them in Chapter 4. It is even more helpful if you take a deep, slow breath as you say the affirmation to yourself. The deep breath helps you relax.

This technique takes some practice and you may need to use it many times in the course of a day for a particularly dominant worry thought. However, if each time you worry you use this technique, gradually it will recede into the background and you'll need to use the technique less often.

Some people have found the "Scarlett O'Hara technique" to be a great aid in overcoming these obsessive thoughts. (Scarlett O'Hara was the heroine in *Gone with the Wind* who handled her problems by saying to herself, "I'll think about that tomorrow.") To try this for yourself you will need a small notebook or pad of paper (and pen or pencil) that you can keep with you at all times. If at any time throughout the day you catch yourself starting to worry about something, pull out your pad and jot it down. As you write, say to yourself as Scarlett O'Hara did, "I'll think about that tomorrow." To be fair with yourself, designate a period each day, perhaps 15 to 30 minutes, to review your worry list and give it your undivided attention. Concentrated worry is more productive than worry that is slipped in among your normal daily activities. As you become better at this, you will notice you are able to complete your worry in less and less time, until one day you'll notice you don't seem to be spending any time on worry!

One caution with the Scarlett O'Hara technique. This is not a blanket permission to those of you who procrastinate. Taking action is the best approach to handling procrastination. Also, for those 10 percent of the cases in which what you're worried about probably will happen and you can do something about it, you need to go beyond the circular, nonproductive worry process and move yourself to take action. Whether your action is successful or not is less important than your doing something. As soon as you begin to act, you regain some control over your life. In that respect, worry and procrastination are very similar. The only way out of procrastination is to get started on the task, no matter how small or insignificant the start. The act of starting breaks its stranglehold. So it is with worry. Initiating some action, no matter how small, will help you reduce stress and restore your personal power. The manager who is struggling with which candidate to choose might check references rather than agonize over whether or not he is making the right decision. If the situation turns out to be your worst-case scenario, do something to reduce your fear or something to strengthen your ability to cope.

Each of these strategies can help you overcome worry, although each takes time and effort. Remember that to take no action will leave you in the same place 6 months or 6 years from now. Melody Beattie in *Codependent No More* says bluntly, "Worry and obsession constitute mental abuse. Stop doing those things."[5] If you begin today to change some of the things that are causing you stress, including worry, your life can be very different in just a few short months.

HANDLE YOUR ANGER

It is a normal response to be disappointed when things do not happen the way you want them to. Thus if you are faced with a situation you cannot change, disappointment can be expected. Often anger will accompany disappointment, although it is not usually helpful.

If you travel by plane you have probably seen examples of nonproductive anger. Jack was in the Memphis airport waiting for a connection that was delayed owing to bad weather. He had already been there four hours when he heard some yelling and a string of obscenities. He turned to see another passenger, red in the face and fists clenched, screaming at the ticket agent about the delay. The ticket agent was trying to be as calm and polite as possible in that situation, but it was easy to see he too was upset. Jack just chuckled to himself, "Doesn't that guy realize all the yelling in the world won't change the weather?" A little while later Jack approached the ticket counter and expressed his concern over the behavior of the other passenger. The ticket agent smiled and said, "Well, I decide who gets first option on the few available seats on the next flight." Then Jack calmly requested a meal voucher since he had now been in the airport five hours, and the ticket agent pleasantly complied.

In this situation, how could anger help? It couldn't. The upset passenger raised his blood pressure, embarrassed himself in front of others, and lessened his chances of getting what he wanted—a flight out of Memphis. Of course he wanted to be on his way; so did all the other passengers. Once he realized he could not change the situation, though, anything he did to delay accepting reality only increased his stress.

Recall a time when you were angry. Did the anger help you? Did it reduce the stress you felt at the time, or did it worsen the level of stress you were experiencing? If you are honest with yourself, you probably will say the anger did not help the situation.

Anger is what is known as a secondary emotion. That means it comes second, after another feeling—usually hurt or fear. Anger tends to mask these more vulnerable feelings from ourselves and from others. To be able to accept the things you cannot change means you will need to come to terms with these underlying feelings. When they are protected by anger, it takes longer. First the anger needs to be resolved, then you can resolve the underlying feelings, and finally reach acceptance.

Ironically, anger does not protect you quite as well as you might think. Research studies have monitored the effect of anger on the body. Rather than protecting you, it actually weakens the immune system. In *Love, Medicine, and Miracles,* Bernie Siegel writes, "Scientists who have studied responses to stress have found that ineffectual anger is the emotion most destructive to homeostasis. A serene acceptance of *what is* promotes health, but by keeping the mind clear it also puts a person in a better position to change things that need changing."[6]

Think about a situation when you felt angry. As you bring that image vividly into your mind, notice how you feel. Are your muscles getting tense? Can you feel your jaw starting to tighten? Is your heart racing? How do you feel emotionally? Are you aware of becoming upset or anxious inside? These are the common responses to anger.

If you use these feelings as a signal that you need to take action, anger can be productive. When you notice yourself feeling angry, you want to accept the feeling for what it is, express it or let go of it, and gently move on. Too often when you notice feelings of anger, you take no action. Instead you replay what you are angry about over and over, keeping yourself perpetually upset and stressed.

Acceptance paves the way for new action and facilitates managing the stressor. When Jack accepted that his flight was going to be delayed several hours, he freed himself to act. Did he want to read a book, do some paperwork, make phone calls, or talk with other passengers? He was free to move on and go ahead with his life. His angry fellow passenger lost all those hours in emotion. He was not able to choose to act and his energy was consumed by *reaction.*

If you are aware of feeling anger, what specifically can you do to get rid of it? There are several things you can do. You can start by looking underneath it for the primary feeling. What is scaring or threatening you? Who or what hurt you? Do you feel helpless or powerless? This may not be easy to identify at first because you want to protect yourself from this pain. However, if you continue to mull over these questions, the answer will become apparent. Often this will dissolve the anger because you see what you were trying to protect.

If the anger is directed toward another person, you may want to express it. A four-step model that works very well follows.

Step one. Express how you are feeling. Own up to the angry or upset feelings. To do this, you will use an *I* statement, which was discussed in Chapter 2 pp. 54–57 in the DEAR approach to confronting someone. You could start with the simple phrase, I feel angry. . . .

Step two. Explain briefly what the situation is that is upsetting you. Be as objective as you can. This is not the time to blame or attack someone, nor is it the time for a 30-minute discussion of the situation. Keep it short, simple, and direct. For example, you could say, I feel angry *when you criticize me in a team meeting.* . . .

Step three. This is the tough part. Now you are going to expose the underlying feeling that is causing the anger. With this step you take the risk of letting the other person know what your true feelings are. Remember, anger is a secondary emotion that is protecting you from your vulnerable feelings of hurt or fear. This step is the most powerful of this four-step process. Most people drop their defensiveness and hostility toward others when someone shows their true feelings. As you become more practiced with this step, you will discover you feel anger less often because you will learn to notice the primary feelings earlier and express them directly without masking them with anger. For example, you might say, I feel angry when you criticize me in a team meeting *because I fear my co-workers won't respect me.*

Step four. Ask for a specific remedy to your hurt or fear. For example, you might say, I feel angry when you criticize me in a team meeting because I fear my co-workers won't respect me. *In the future, if you have a criticism of me, please say it in private.* Not only does step four resolve the specific situation, it can often prevent the situation from recurring.

Let's look at an example of this process in action. Glenn's company has redesigned its offices and now, instead of a private office, he has a cubicle. Glenn is mad about this change and tells anyone who will listen to him. It has been three weeks now and although other people seem to be adapting to the change, he is still mad. He finally realizes that others are beginning to tire of his constant complaining, so he decides to try this process. The most difficult part is step three, in which he tries to figure out why he is so mad. Of what could he be afraid? Nothing comes to mind. What or who has hurt him? As he ponders this question, it comes to him. He feels hurt that his work as a personnel specialist has not been considered worthy of a private office. Glenn feels the information about salary and benefits he is providing to job applicants is confidential. He doesn't feel comfortable talking about these issues when he knows someone in the next cubicle can overhear him. With this awareness, he schedules an appointment with his boss to discuss the problem.

"Peter, I feel upset about losing my enclosed office for a cubicle. Much of the work I do is confidential. I feel uncomfortable discussing salary information with candidates when I know people in the adjoining cubicles can overhear our conversation. I need your help in coming up with a way to do my job and still ensure the confidentiality of each interview."

In this example, Glenn has accepted his cubicle as his office and is able to go beyond it to take action to get his needs met. There are any number of solutions he and his boss may try—from getting a machine that produces white noise for confidentiality, to giving Glen access to a private office or conference room where he can meet with candidates.

Like other emotions, once anger is identified and expressed, it tends to disappear. Don't let anger prevent you from accepting the things you cannot change.

DON'T MAKE IT WORSE

When you don't like a situation, you may engage in a variety of counterproductive behaviors to avoid accepting reality. We just discussed anger, which is one such behavior, but there are others. These are all "copers," quick fixes that give short-term relief with long-term price tags.

Resentment

When you refuse to express your anger or let go of it, you build up resentments and hold grudges. You actually give your power to other people because you stay upset about something they did or said. The other people are not suffering! They may not even know you are upset. This passive emotion suppresses the immune system.

Complaining

It is not pleasant to listen to a constant complainer. Don't let yourself fall into this category. Complaining is a passive reaction that does not give you any control. It is a reactive response that results in feelings of helplessness. The mind-set is one of wishful thinking. That is, if you complain long enough or to the right people, something will be done. Complaining will not change bad weather, nor will it change modular furniture into private offices. It keeps your emotions stirred up, with no chance of resolution. Replace complaining with acceptance of the situation and a plan of action.

Revenge

You have no doubt heard the expression, "Don't get mad; get even." Neither getting mad nor getting even will resolve stress. Plotting revenge against a person or a company keeps you embroiled emotionally, without any release from the stress. Revenge does not solve problems; it is an indirect means of addressing conflict. Be mature enough to express yourself and get on with your life. There is another axiom that is true: "What goes around comes around." Your negative behavior will come back to haunt you. Remember that if the other party is in the wrong, he or she is also subject to this universal principle.

Gossip

Company gossip can fall anywhere on a wide continuum, from interesting and relatively harmless to malicious. Don't allow yourself to criticize other people behind their backs. If you are upset, use one of the skills outlined for expressing anger or handling conflict. Like the other negative coping strategies we've discussed, gossip does not remove the stress, but keeps it churning inside you. Focus on ways to disagree with a person's ideas without attacking the person. Discuss the situation directly with the individual rather than feeding the rumor mill.

Work Slowdowns

Some people, when they feel stress due to an interpersonal conflict or an unpopular decision, make a deliberate effort to lower their productivity. This is much like revenge and similarly will come back to haunt you. When you know you are giving less than your best effort, you lower your self-esteem. This behavior does nothing to change the stressor. As a coping mechanism, such an action has a short-term benefit before the long-term costs start accumulating.

Self-Pity

Feeling sorry for yourself will not change the situation, nor will it make you feel any better. When you feel self-pity, you give away your power and assume a helpless role in the situation. It is perfectly okay to feel bad or disappointed when things do not go your way; to continue feeling bad isolates you and adds to the stress you were already feeling.

SUMMARY

In summary, there are some things you cannot change. You need to accept reality instead of trying to fight it. This gentle act is empowering in that as you focus on the present, you stop worrying about the past or the future. Reactive strategies may *feel* like a release from stress, but in the long term they lead to increased stress. These short-term strategies include negative thoughts, worry, anger, resentment, complaining, revenge, attacking, self-pity, and work slowdowns. Don't let them stop you from being honest with yourself about current reality and accepting what is.

Chapter Four

The L of CALM: Let Go

You probably know more about "holding on" and "adding on" than you know about "letting go." This causes you a great deal of stress. In this chapter you'll explore how you can begin the gentle process of letting go of your attachments to negative beliefs, unrealistic expectations, dysfunctional relationships, and unreasonable commitments. When you do, you'll free yourself for more creativity and enjoyment in your life.

HOLDING ON

This occurs when you attempt to maintain everything in your life exactly as it is, even though it may no longer be useful or productive. This is often seen when someone is promoted from a line worker to a manager. The new manager moves into a different role and still holds on to former responsibilities. Rather than training someone to take over the previous job, he holds on to control. Take the case of Jeff, who started with a small manufacturing firm at an entry-level position. Over the years he moved up the ranks until he became manager of manufacturing. He was responsible for revenues of over $60 million and yet people within the company could not change offices

111

without his approval! He was still making decisions that would have been better made by lower levels of management.

This also occurs with entrepreneurial ventures. In the early days the entrepreneur or founder needs to do everything, but as the company grows she needs to let go and assign these tasks to others. Some insist on holding on, to their personal and corporate detriment.

Sadly, many people choose to hold on to past disappointments, frustrations, or disagreements with others. This keeps them locked in the past instead of in the present. As discussed in Chapter 3, whenever you lose sight of the present by focusing on either the past or the future, you are inviting stress. This type of holding on creates stress for others because of the tension that surrounds keeping grudges, disappointments, or frustrations alive.

Pat, who worked in a financial institution, held on to every negative experience she had, not only in her professional life but also in her personal life. In the cafeteria she was the first to recount how she was mistreated, passed over, or misunderstood. Just the mention of certain people's names was enough to send her off on a tirade. Pat never seemed to have a good day or be happy. Colleagues knew that crossing her was the same as initiating a cold war. She suffered from ulcers and felt perpetually upset, uptight, and angry. Too bad she couldn't let go of some of those petty grievances and release herself from the upset she was feeling.

Most holding on occurs in these areas: feelings, beliefs, expectations, things, people, and the body.

Feelings

You experience a range of feelings during the day. To some of these feelings you assign positive labels, and to others you assign negative labels. Thus you arbitrarily decide that one feeling is more desirable than another. The reality, of course, is that a feeling is a feeling, nothing more or less. A wide range of feelings makes up the human experience. Just as there can be no darkness without light, there can be no joy without sadness.

Therefore, it is not feelings that create problems or stress. Rather, it is the meanings you assign to feelings and how attached you become to those meanings.

Craig learned this through some painful experiences. While at a departmental meeting, he became angry with his vice president. The two of them exchanged harsh words and afterwards Craig felt bad. On another day he got into a dispute with a client about a bill. The client protested the bill was wrong and became loud and rude. Craig left the encounter feeling hurt and angry himself. On another occasion someone from the office "borrowed" one of his files and did not return it. Craig spent over an hour tracking it down. He felt disgusted that someone would take something without asking. After a period of time he found himself increasingly upset and distressed about such incidents until he became depressed and disillusioned with people in general.

He was describing this to a friend when the friend said, "You know, Craig, it's as if you're constantly dragging around a big bag of bones. Every time something happens that disappoints you, doesn't meet your expectations, or hurts you, you pick it up like a bone and throw it in the bag. After all these years you're carrying an awfully heavy bag. In fact I can see it is literally weighing you down. If I were you, I'd do two things. First, I would stop collecting bones! Second, I would look in that bag and pull out a few and throw them away! No one is suffering except you. Most of those hurts you carry around are known only to yourself."

Craig gave these comments considerable thought and decided his friend was right. He made a promise to himself not to add any more bones to his bag and to systematically throw out all the bones he had been carrying.

How many bad feelings do you carry around? To let go of them means you will need to forgive others. Don't get mad, and don't get even—release the feelings; let go of them. Holding on and carrying them with you can only make you feel bad and will do nothing to change the situation. A colleague may have just been informed that an account was lost when you walked in to make a request. Thus she snaps at you and you leave feeling hurt and angry. Stop. Let go of the hurt and anger and forgive that person for being short-tempered. You will feel better and have more to offer the next person you meet. If you hold the anger, you keep yourself upset by replaying the unpleasant situation over and over in your mind. When you do this, you're living in the past, not the present.

Forgiveness, like acceptance (Chapter 3), is deceptive; it is an active process that puts you in control. You may be surprised to discover how many bad feelings you hold on to. Forgiveness lightens your load, reduces your stress, and reduces the stress of others around you.

Remember that this is step three of the CALM model. In step one you change the things you can, which might mean asserting your rights with another person. It might mean confronting someone about how his or her behavior is affecting you. At step one you may get a change in behavior that solves the problem. You would not need to progress through the model. If there is no change after you confront someone, you may need to accept the situation for what it is. Then in step three, instead of holding on to negative feelings about the situation, let go of them and forgive the other person and yourself.

To be CALM is more than a series of techniques. It is a philosophy of life. It is an integrated approach to how you live your life. The objective is to keep you as centered, balanced, and powerful as you can be. You empower yourself in the first step of the model by taking action to create the kinds of circumstances you prefer. Simultaneously, you recognize that you are not running the universe. Things will happen that you didn't plan for and don't like. Will you choose to accept and blend with them or will you struggle and resist? It is the contention of this book that struggle and resistance heighten stress, compromise your balance, and threaten your overall well-being. Resistance is directly correlated to holding on. It is easy to become attached to your personal worldview. If you think you have the one true answer, the one right way, then you close down your openness to the world and new learning. You cease to be a traveler on life's journey. It's as if you have already mastered and know everything. Letting go opens the possibility that something new can be learned or added. George Leonard in his book *Mastery* tells the following Zen tale.

> [A] wise man comes to the Zen master, haughty in his great wisdom, asking how he can become even wiser. The master simply pours tea into the wise man's cup and keeps pouring until the cup runs over and spills all over the wise man, letting him know without words that if one's cup is already full, there is no space in it for anything new.[1]

Peace of mind is a feeling that there won't be room for if you are busy holding on to feelings of anger, disappointment, resentment, or hurt.

Beliefs

In Chapter 3 we discussed Ellis's model of how beliefs can cause feelings. You may be holding on to beliefs that do not serve you well. In some cases, what you believe comes from childhood programming and may not even be true! Your belief systems, when they are not consistent with reality, can be a source of stress for you if you become attached to them. Let's look at an example.

Hiro was feeling anxious and upset. He had spent years working with audiovisual equipment, including video equipment. His company had secured some film, taken by a local television station, of one of the company plants in operation. Hiro was going to edit it to create an employee-training film. After noting what excerpts he wanted to use, he set up the dubbing equipment. When he finished transferring the film, he rewound it and discovered he had pressed "record" instead of "play." Not only did he not have the excerpts for his training film, he had erased the original! For a week Hiro nearly made himself sick with worry, wondering how he could ever tell his boss. He couldn't believe he could make such a dumb mistake. He was an expert with video equipment; how could he have pushed the wrong button?

People make mistakes. No one is perfect. Hiro had a belief that because he was trained and experienced, he should not make a mistake. In his mind, there was no excuse or explanation for his error. It was this belief that was upsetting him more than the lost tape. To expect yourself to be perfect is what Dr. Albert Ellis would call an irrational belief. When you notice yourself feeling disproportionately stressed or upset about a situation, you can bet there is an irrational belief operating.

You may recognize some of these more common irrational beliefs.

1. You must have love and approval from all people.
2. You must be totally competent, adequate, and achieving.
3. You have to view things as awful, horrible, or terrible when you are frustrated, treated unfairly, or rejected.
4. Unhappiness comes from factors outside your control and you can't control them.

  5. If something seems frightening or scary, you should dwell on it as if it will occur.

  6. It is easier to avoid than to face life's difficulties.

  7. Your past is all important and should affect your present life.

This is only the beginning of a list of irrational beliefs. You carry your own internal set of beliefs that creates stress for you. Can you identify them?

As you become attached to these beliefs, you begin to expect the world to operate in compliance with them. If it does not, you experience stress. Marta's experience is a good example.

Marta believed in the Golden Rule—"Do unto others as you would have others do unto you." Consequently, whenever she went out for lunch, she asked if anyone in the office would like her to bring something back for them. Over time she began to feel resentful; no one ever asked her if she wanted something when they went out. She expected them to behave as she did and check with her before they went to lunch. When they didn't, she felt used and angry.

Can you see how Marta used her beliefs to create expectations? She attached meaning to the fact that her expectations weren't met, saying something like, "Those people are inconsiderate," and she felt bad. A better approach would be for Marta to use her assertive skills to take charge of her life by asking her colleagues directly for what she wants.

In Chapter 3, you learned about several types of negative thinking, including *shoulds,* that can create stress. Whenever you say the word *should,* there is an underlying belief. As an experiment, notice your *shoulds* for the rest of the day and see if you can identify the underlying beliefs. Then, ask yourself if those beliefs are based on reality. Here are a few examples to get you started.

Should	I should have gotten the Carter account.
Belief	I need to be totally competent at everything I do.
Should	I should have finished this monthly report an hour ago!
Belief	It's awful to feel frustrated.
Should	I should have called when I knew I was running late.
Belief	I need everyone to approve of me.

Now add your own to the list. Your irrational beliefs may be different from those Ellis described. That's okay. The purpose is to begin to recognize what your beliefs are.

Should _____

Belief _____

What can you do when these dysfunctional beliefs begin to create unnecessary stress? Let go of them and begin to replace them with more realistic beliefs. Using the examples above, you can convert the beliefs into preferences instead of commands.

Belief	I need to be totally competent at everything I do.
Revised	I like to feel competent; it feels good. Although I would like to be competent at everything I do, I realize and accept that this is not possible.
Belief	It's awful to feel frustrated.
Revised	I would prefer not to feel frustrated. However, the reality is that I will be frustrated from time to time. I don't need to view frustration as terrible; I can accept that this is how I feel.
Belief	I need everyone to approve of me.

Revised   I prefer to be liked, although I realize not
                everyone will like me. I can't guarantee
                that everyone will like me no matter what
                I do.

Now see if you can revise your unreasonable beliefs
into more rational preferences. Once you begin to see
preferences or wants instead of demands, you dramati-
cally reduce your internal stress.

Belief _____

Revised _____

Remember when you completed Braham's Work Stress
Inventory (Chapter 1)? Although external events may be
the source of some of the stress in your life, by far the
greatest source of stress is your internal belief system and
resultant self-talk. Some people who suffer physically
from stress have practically no external stressors. Their
symptoms come directly from their unreasonable beliefs.
External stressors are exponentially worsened when there
are irrational beliefs operating.

Examine your beliefs, and change those that create
stress for you.

Expectations

Most people make some effort to plan their lives, whether
that takes the form of a daily *To Do* list, or whether it's a
long-term set of life goals. Planning is a valuable activity
that gives your actions direction and focus. However, if
you hold rigidly to those plans and let them become expectations, you may create stress for yourself.

Conrad came into work with a clear plan of what he
wanted to accomplish. He had prepared his *To Do* list the
night before. Within the first half-hour there was a glitch
in his plan. His secretary was out ill, so the mailing he
planned to get out was going to have to wait. Then the

computer locked up and he couldn't access the information he needed to complete a priority project. He could feel himself getting more and more upset and stressed.

What was the cause of Conrad's stress? Was it the ill secretary or the computer? No, those are life's unexpected events that get thrown at you. The real source of his stress was his holding on to his expectations for the day. Rather than let them go and create a new plan for the day, Conrad held on to them and became increasingly frustrated. He needed to flow with the changing circumstances of his day to manage his stress. Instead he became a victim of his expectations.

Sometimes it is more than mere expectations that cause stress. It is unreasonable expectations. For example, do you expect yourself to be able to make a 20-minute drive between meetings in 10 minutes? That isn't reasonable and you're going to feel stress. During the holidays do you expect yourself to work all day, maintain the home, decorate, shop, bake, send holiday greeting cards, entertain, and enjoy time with your family? That's unreasonable. Yet people hold these expectations every year. Let go of some of those expectations. Decide what is most important to you, focus on that, and let the rest go. Stop trying to be Superman or Superwoman. Stop trying to please everyone else; choose health and peace of mind instead.

As soon as you attach yourself to your expectations, you lose your ability to accept what is. You try to force reality to comply with your plan, your picture of the way you want things to be. In addition to frustrating yourself, you just may miss out on spontaneous fun. Here's an example.

Rick was flying from Tampa to Kansas City with a change of planes in St. Louis. When he got to St. Louis, a blizzard had just hit. Every outbound flight was first delayed, then canceled. At first he held to his expectation of getting to Kansas City that day, anxiously watching the TV monitors, repeatedly calling his customers in Kansas City with updates. By noon he and several other passengers reached the conclusion they weren't flying anywhere soon. So they let that plan go, boarded a shuttle into the city's downtown, visited some of the sights, booked hotel rooms, and had a wonderful time creating an adventure for themselves. How many others sat in the airport for 18 or more hours, tired, frustrated, angry, or upset?

Last, you may get caught up in rising expectations. Have you ever noticed what happens after a success? There is a tendency to expect yourself to set another, higher goal. And you expect yourself to reach it quicker and more efficiently than the previous one. This continuous demand on yourself to do more, better, faster creates stress. You need to set limits and take care of yourself. Don't let your rising expectations, or society's, stress you.

Managing stress means being flexible and adaptable. It means being willing to let go of your expectations and change your plans when the situation calls for it.

Things

Adults hold on to things, not unlike children do. When parents try to teach a child to share, the child clutches each toy the parent proposes to give away and refuses to let go of it. Some people maintain this behavior long into adulthood. Sara worked for such a man. Everything that came into the office was to be filed. Nothing could be thrown away. The file cabinets were bulging. It was increasingly difficulty to find the important things because of all the unimportant ones Sarah needed to wade through. Sara hated to go into his office; it was the home of a true "pack rat," as she called him. More time was wasted trying to find something on his desk than she cared to admit. She often thought of the joy she'd feel if she came in some Saturday, brought a two-ton Dumpster, and started to pitch things into it!

If Sarah's boss could learn to let go of some of that paper and clutter, he would be more effective and reduce the stress of those around him. In a culture that is dominated by a drive for consumption, many people have more things to care for, protect, and maintain than they need or want. What do you need to let go? Again, the paradox "less is more" applies.

Perhaps the "thing" that you hold on to is work. Do you mentally take your work home with you? Today most people do mental work, not physical labor. If what you did was only physical, it would be relatively easy to leave it at the end of the day, but mental work can go with you while you drive, while you're on vacation, and while you're supposedly "listening" to your partner or children. You need to give yourself a mental break from your work. You might find it helpful to create a ritual that you'll use to separate work from nonwork time. For example, some people lock their appointment book in their desk and tell themselves that they're locking away the day's work as well. Other people create a transition between work and home that helps them leave work where it belongs. The most common transition is some form of exercise, either at a gym or on your own. The physical release facilitates the mental release. Others transition using meditation. These transitions will be described in Chapter 5.

People

You may hold on to people. Mike was this way. He had a couple of guys in the department who weren't really doing their jobs. He had talked with them on several occasions, but nothing seemed to change. They weren't bad guys; in fact they were the nicest employees you could find anywhere. They simply didn't have the skills they needed to do the job. Mike continued to keep them on the payroll, even though others in the department had to do extra work to carry the slack. This created low morale among the people who were always doing a little more than their share. However, Mike thought it wasn't too much to ask when these two guys were so nice and tried so hard.

Has Mike done anyone a favor? No. He is holding on to two nonproductive employees at their own expense and at the expense of the rest of the department. There may be another place in the company where these people could contribute in a meaningful way. If Mike had a department filled with people who could do their jobs, he would increase morale and reduce everyone's stress; but he holds on under the misconception that he is being nice. Meanwhile he too suffers under the pressure of a department that is perpetually behind in its work.

Perhaps you've outgrown some of your friends (or they've outgrown you). It's sad to let them go, yet necessary for your continued development. To hold on will hurt both of you in the long run.

The Body

Did you know that certain body postures can create specific feelings? As an experiment try slumping your shoulders. Drop your head and lower your eyes. Let your arms hang limp and lifeless at your sides. Now walk around like this. Notice how you feel. Did you find yourself feeling low, self-conscious, perhaps even depressed? Those are the feelings associated with that body posture.

Now put your head up. Smile. Stand erect, not rigid but relaxed. Look at the world in front of you and around you as you walk around. Do you notice any change in how you're feeling from the first exercise? Of course. You now feel more energy (for one thing it is easier to breathe standing erect than when you are slumped), and more confident. Probably you also notice yourself feeling more positive.

Most people habitually hold their bodies in certain postures. Some of those are postures of fear or insecurity, anger, or defensiveness. Are you willing to explore the possibility of letting go of your habitual ways of movement for ways that would feel freer and more empowered? You can begin this with the simple process of diaphragmatic breathing. Chapter 5 will tell you how to trade your present shallow breathing for deep breathing that also improves your posture.

To explore further how you may be creating stress by how you hold your body, consider practicing a martial art such as aikido, taking a movement class, or seeing a body awareness therapist. You can change your thoughts and change your body, or you can change your body and change your thoughts. One of these ways will work for you!

Holding on is pervasive. You may hold on to people, things, feelings, beliefs, expectations, or your body. Some of us hold on to all these; others have a favorite one or two. What do you hold on to? How does that create stress for you?

ADDING ON

In addition to holding on, you may "add on." When asked, do you agree to take on new projects, join new committees, or cultivate new clients, in addition to your regular schedule? This works out for a while, but as a long-term strategy it is fraught with stress. Any structure, no matter how strong, can take only so much pressure before it starts to weaken and eventually break. The human body is not exempt from this basic principle. Take Charlie's situation.

Charlie was a star in the company. Bright, likable, and a quick thinker, he was sought out by many others. This flattered Charlie and he usually agreed to help out. One day, though, he noticed heart palpitations and tingling down his arm. When he went to see his family doctor, he was asked to describe his work. Charlie explained that he loved it. He was involved in a number of special projects throughout the company, sat in on most committee meetings, and managed another department while its manager was on short-term disability. Charlie was also on call for the training department people, who used him at least once a quarter for some of their technical training. The doctor looked Charlie directly in the eye after hearing all this and said, "Charlie, if you don't start prioritizing and letting go of some of those commitments, you won't be around for anybody much longer."

Charlie needs to go back to step one of the CALM model and learn to say no. You can change a potentially stressful situation by setting limits instead of adding on.

WHY LET GO?

The process of letting go is simple, yet difficult. It is paradoxical. Letting go is a decision you make and then you allow it to happen. You hold on or add on out of fear. What will be left if you let go? Who will you be without your beliefs or feelings? What will others think if you let go of relationships that no longer serve you? As Marilyn Ferguson says in *The Aquarian Conspiracy*, "It's not so much that we're afraid of change, or so in love with the old ways, but it's that place in between we fear . . . it's like being in between trapezes. It's Linus when his blanket is in the dryer. There's nothing to hold on to."

There is loss associated with whatever you let go. Attendant to loss is grief. Some letting go is easier than others. Letting go of your expectations that you'll be an officer in your company and accepting that you won't progress beyond being a supervisor hurts. Letting go of someone you've mentored when she's ready to be independent of you is sad. Whether you choose to hold on or let go, the path is not easy. One road, the less-traveled road of letting go, helps you stay balanced and manage your stress. The other road gives you the illusion of control but higher levels of stress.

When you emotionally attach yourself to beliefs, people, things, feelings, or expectations, you make letting go that much tougher. As discussed in Chapter 3, situations in and of themselves are neither positive nor negative; they exist. Period. You give each situation, each interaction with another human being, and each thought you think all its meaning. The meaning comes from nowhere else. Why do you dread Mondays and celebrate Fridays? There is no reason other than the meaning you choose to give each of those days. Why do you become upset with yourself if you make a mistake? Because you have attached meaning to doing things right. Why do you stay upset for months after losing a promotion? Because you've attached your self-esteem to the promotion. Only one person gives these situations their meaning—you. In the following example, see how Connie created stress for herself because of her attachments to people.

The cake had been brought out, party horns were blowing, and everyone was celebrating—everyone that is, except Connie. She felt like running away or crying. Two of her key employees were retiring. They had been with the company for over 25 years. What would she do? The department just couldn't run without them. They knew so much of the company's history and so many reasons why things were done as they were. They had given her so much support. Connie felt abandoned and depressed.

Did Connie need to experience this much stress? No. It is sad to see longtime employees leave. Their friendship and their contributions to the department will be missed. However, is it the end of the department or of productive work relationships? No. Connie has attached herself to these people. By giving their leaving such significance, she upsets herself. If she can let go of them while remembering the good times and their contributions, she can move on without the overwhelming stress.

To let go of attachments is to face the reality that things change all the time. To hold on to what is, hoping to keep it the same, is to guarantee disappointment and stress. Each moment gives way to the next. In every ending there is a beginning—another paradox. Your ability to grow is directly proportionate to your ability to let go. Your ability to stay calm and relaxed is directly proportionate to your ability to let go. Imagine yourself grabbing a handful of sand and holding it tightly in your fist. What will happen to the sand? It will all trickle through your fingers. The tighter you try to hold on, the less sand you will have. If you want to keep the sand, you need to let go. Open your fist and hold your palm open. The sand stays in your hand when you let go of the tight, rigid, clenched fist. You enact this drama every day, often all day. You habitually hold your breath, cling to past feelings, unrealistic expectations, and so on, all in a misguided effort to control your stress. If you can loosen your grip just a little—let go—you'll discover that you capture relaxation, calm, and peace.

If you are going to climb a ladder, there is only one way to get to the top. You will need to let go of the rung you are holding before you can reach for the next one. The principle is the same whether it's an aluminum ladder or a career ladder!

People who do not learn to let go and release themselves from stress can and do burn out. The outcome is that they are forced to let go. Sadly, they may let go of their jobs, their health, their relationships with others, and their self-esteem. When you reach the burnout stage, you do not choose what you will let go. It is out of your control. How much better it is to learn to let go along the way, to keep the choices within your power, and to prevent burnout. One way or the other, you will let go, and it is your choice to either control the process or let it control you.

When you begin to let go of your attachments, you will make a discovery: You will feel a profound sense of freedom. There won't be so much "noise" in your life. There will be space for solitude. You need some moments of quiet for yourself. You need time to think, time to create, and time to renew yourself. Solitude can provide this.

How often have you said or thought, I can't hear myself think? You can hear your thoughts only when you simplify your life enough that you have time to listen. That's what letting go does. It starts to simplify things. You can see more clearly when the clutter is out of the way. Once you begin to let go, not only will you benefit by reducing your stress, you'll also discover you're practicing a spiritual discipline.

Balancing

When you are holding on or adding on, your life can get out of balance. You add more work commitments and suddenly notice you have become estranged from your family. You hold on to old methods and procedures for doing things at the office and realize you're out of touch with the present; you may be passed over for promotions.

Balance is a delicate and ongoing process. If you tip it, you will pay a price physically, emotionally, mentally, or spiritually. The body's natural state is to be in balance. When that is disrupted, the body will adapt in an effort to restore itself. That adaptation, as you learned in Chapter 1, often comes in the form of symptoms. In fact, if you are experiencing symptoms, it is helpful to view them as the body's attempt to communicate with you—to tell you that you are no longer in balance. If you heed this message, you can take action to assist the body to regain its balance and thereby reduce your stress. The more you close your ears, either by refusing to pay attention to the message or by medicating it away so that you can't hear it any longer, the more you force your body to escalate its adaptation efforts.

Solitude helps you restore balance. It is the purposeful choice, rather than the body's imposition, of down time. Through solitude you can learn to create a place of quiet within you that you can access whenever you need it. You can literally let go of the pressures of the moment to retreat to your inner place where you can think through what you need to do. Chapter 5 describes some ways to create this solitude. Without this you will react, adjust, and cope with stress, rather than following the CALM model and managing the stress.

With time for solitude you come to know yourself better; you can differentiate between what you want and need and what someone else wants or expects you to do. You gain greater control over your own life through clarity about what you value. You can more easily make choices about what's important.

Letting go has two levels of benefits. On one level you do not hold onto stressors or add new ones. This gives you some time for yourself—an opportunity to experience some moments of solitude in which you can continue to clarify what is important in your life, and where you want to invest your limited time and energies. The second benefit is that you are more able to stay in the present and experience a physical and emotional freedom that is not possible when you rigidly cling to people, things, beliefs, or expectations. The process enables you to restore balance to your life, which is critical to health and well-being. Letting go is the single best way to prevent burnout. Your ability to be present is directly related to your willingness to let go.

TYPE A BEHAVIOR

In Chapter 1 you learned that much of your stress is self-imposed. Over the years you've developed some habits and behaviors that increase your stress. Some of those behaviors, such as worry and perfectionism, we've explored how to change. There are other behaviors you may want to let go.

In the 1950s, Dr. Meyer Friedman first identified what is now referred to as *Type A behavior*. Research studies since then have consistently shown Type A individuals to be 50 percent more vulnerable to heart disease than Type B persons. According to Dr. Friedman's research, people with Type B behavior can practically be guaranteed they will not suffer a heart attack before age 60 or 65. Type As can be given no such guarantee.

To find out what your stress personality is, ask yourself these questions:

1. Do you try to be on time for all meetings and appointments?
2. Would you describe yourself as competitive?
3. Do you like to do several things at the same time, like talk on the phone and read your mail?
4. Do you feel rushed most of the time?
5. Do you do things fast—for instance, walk fast, talk fast, or eat fast?
6. Do you spend most of your time at work to the exclusion of other activities?

7. Do you feel upset if you have to wait—whether in line, for traffic, or for an appointment?

8. Do you try to achieve many poorly defined goals?

If you answered yes to four or more questions, you're exhibiting behavior typical of a Type A person. Less than four yes answers is more typical of Type B.

The Type A personality is composed of a cluster of behaviors including competitiveness, hurry sickness, and aggressiveness or hostility. Studies over the years have tried to isolate just which characteristics are most responsible for health-related problems. For a time it was believed that suppressed anger was the key culprit. A 1992 study by Dr. Joann Manson of Brigham and Women's Hospital in Boston concludes that it is the cluster of Type A behaviors and not just anger. She found that Type As had lower amounts of HDL (high-density lipoprotein), which is the "good" cholesterol. Lower levels of HDL increase your risk for heart attack. Further research is needed to clarify the relationship between Type A behavior and HDL and to give a definitive answer as to which behaviors increase the risk.

Just what causes Type A behavior is not completely clear, although there does seem to be a relationship between low self-esteem and the behavior.

Low Self-Esteem

How you feel about yourself is the way you measure self-esteem. The more you like and accept yourself, the higher your self-esteem. Sadly, many people do not like themselves very much. Consequently they engage in any number of behaviors to compensate for the low opinion they hold of themselves.

For example, some people go out of their way to "do good and be nice." The logic is that if they are good enough people, they will like themselves and, in the interim at least, others will also like them. They are frequently taken advantage of because it is difficult for them to say no.

Some people boast about their accomplishments, who they know, what they own, or where they've been. They try to project an air of importance. They think that if others think they are important, others will like them and in the process they may come to like themselves. However, they are usually perceived as arrogant or egotistical. Self-acceptance rarely results.

Others with low self-esteem try to hide from the world and not be noticed. They experience feelings of worthlessness and do not feel they deserve to be included or treated with respect. They have trouble expressing how they feel or what they want.

Some people express their low self-esteem by putting themselves in situations in which they are mistreated, abused, or punished. They seem to want to show the world just how "bad" they really are. They expect to be treated like the "not-okay" people they believe themselves to be. These people are many of society's misfits and victims.

Still others seek to feel okay about themselves through accomplishment. In their minds, the more they are able to achieve the more worthy they are. If they can just achieve enough, they will be graced with the "I'm okay" feeling. This incessant drive to do more, achieve more, and accomplish more underlies Type A behavior, and leads to stress.

However low self-esteem is expressed, it hurts you. While we are most concerned in this book about the person who copes with low self-esteem through doing, achieving, and accomplishing, the following suggestions can help you feel better about yourself no matter how your low self-esteem manifests itself.

Affirmations.   We talked in Chapter 3 about negative self-talk and how it can create stress for you. If you decide to change that self-talk, you will need to replace it with something else, something more positive—affirmations.

An affirmation is a positive statement you say to yourself that affirms you. It builds you up rather than tears you down. It is phrased positively, in terms of what you want, not what you don't want. An example will show the difference.

"I am healthy."

"I don't want to get sick."

In the second example, you do not have an affirmation because it is worded for what you don't want instead of what you want. The wording is very important because the mind does not recognize negatives. The mind works in pictures. When you describe what you don't want, the mind pictures it. What do you see when you say, I don't want to get sick? Most people see someone lying in bed—not a positive image. Now what happens when you say, I am healthy? Do you see someone well-toned and strong engaged in an outdoor sport or activity? As you are beginning to see, the two expressions seem to mean the same thing but are very different in the mind's eye.

When you create your affirmation, put it in the present tense as if it has already occurred. This is a powerful technique for the mind, which does not know the difference between imagination and reality. It responds as if everything told to it in the present tense were true. Then behavior begins to shift gently to align itself with the thoughts or beliefs. You want to use this capacity of the mind to get the outcomes you want with affirmations. Thus you would say "I am healthy," instead of "I want to be healthy" or "I will be healthy."

When you think negative thoughts, your mind uses this process to bring negative outcomes into reality. You may have heard this referred to as the self-fulfilling prophecy. For example, when you use negative thinking such as overgeneralization, you may say something like, "I never get promoted." With this message for the mind to work with, it goes about the process of bringing that statement into reality. Imagine the change if instead of saying, "I never get promoted," you began to say "I am successful." By putting it in the present tense, over time you will begin to behave as if you are successful, instead of behaving as if you will never get promoted. Remember, even things that are not yet true, if said positively and in the present tense, have a better chance of coming true than if you said them negatively. Affirmations mobilize the mind's capacity to create reality.

To be most effective, affirmations need to be said at least twice a day—morning and night—and more often, if you can remember to say them. When you say them to yourself, try to put as much feeling and emotion into them as you can. The mind listens more readily to emotion than to a dull monotone. If you doubt this, ask yourself if you'd rather listen to a dry, boring speaker or an enthusiastic, excited speaker.

If you do this every day for a period of a few months, you will be amazed at how different you feel about yourself. A list of some possible stress-management affirmations follows. Don't choose more than two or three to start. After you master them, you can add others.

I am calm and relaxed.

I manage my stress.

I manage my time.

I am confident.

I release all negative thoughts.

I calmly solve problems.

I'm getting better every day.

I feel at ease with myself.

I let go of irrational beliefs easily.

Daily acknowledgments. If you're like most people, you have a video camera running in your mind all day, recording everything that happens to you. Then at the end of the day, before you go to bed, do you notice that you rewind your video of the day and replay it for yourself? Unfortunately, when most people review their day, they focus on the negatives. You recite the errors you made in speech, behavior, and judgment. You think about what you said that you wished you hadn't said and what you didn't do that you planned to do. This reinforces in your mind the exact behaviors you would like to reduce or eliminate. It makes you feel bad about yourself and amounts to a systematic process of daily destruction. As Dorothy Briggs says in *Celebrate Yourself*, you're either in the building business or the wrecking business. And if you review your shortcomings every night—you're in the wrecking business.

Instead of reviewing your shortcomings, at the end of the day make a list of 10 things about which you feel good. This does not need to be a list of major achievements, but simply a recounting of the day's activities and things that you thought went well. Kindnesses you showed, decisions you made, commitments you honored—anything you did that you think is positive goes on the list.

Like using affirmations, if you begin daily acknowledgments today and use them over a period of a few months, you will be astonished at how your attention has shifted from failures to successes. You will also be amazed at how easily you can see your successes and how many more of them there are.

Self-improvement or self-development? Have you ever been on a self-improvement campaign, trying to make yourself a better person? Most people have at one time or another. Unfortunately, the strategy doesn't work very well. If you've ever done any major remodeling or restored a home, you'll understand why.

When Barbara and her husband bought their 1892 Victorian home, they thought that with a little paint and wallpaper everything would be fine. They were fortunate to be so naive! The first room they chose to work on had large pieces of wallpaper peeling off the walls. Barbara thought to herself, "If I can just get the paper stripped and these walls freshly painted, this room will look great."

Months later the walls were stripped, the plaster repaired, and a fresh coat of paint applied. However, when Barbara went into her room to admire her work, she didn't notice the walls. What she noticed was the woodwork. There was lots of it! A beautiful oak mantlepiece around the fireplace, sliding pocket doors, large baseboards, carved door frames—all painted, and the paint had yellowed over the years and was chipped in places. Barbara thought to herself, "This room will never look right until that woodwork is stripped and returned to its original beauty." The project was slow. It was over a year before all the woodwork was stripped, stained, varnished, and returned to its deserved grandeur.

Barbara expected to be pleased when she stepped back to admire her work. However, she didn't notice the freshly painted walls, nor did she notice the beautifully restored woodwork. Her eye lighted on the floor. It was hardwood, stained and clearly in need of more than a cleaning. It needed to be sanded, restained, and varnished—another time-consuming project.

When the floor was finished, do you think Barbara was satisfied? No. You see, no matter what she did, it only served to magnify something else that needed to be done. And that's precisely what happens with your self-esteem when you start on a self-improvement campaign. You identify something that needs to be "fixed" about yourself—your codependency, an addiction, or a compulsive behavior. You may work months or years to solve the problem. When you finally do resolve it, are you satisfied with yourself and do you now have high self-esteem? Not necessarily. More likely, growth in one area of your life has magnified problems in others. Rather than feeling high self-esteem, likely you still feel many "not-okay" feelings.

What's the solution? Are you supposed to ignore the parts of yourself that need changing to avoid the self-improvement trap? No. There is another solution—self-development.

Self-development takes an approach opposite to self-improvement. While self-improvement starts from the premise that something is wrong and needs to be fixed, self-development starts from the premise that something is right and can be leveraged or enhanced. In other words, instead of focusing on your weaknesses, you start with your talents or gifts. Identify your strengths. Then ask yourself, How could I develop that gift? How could I more fully utilize that talent? How could I leverage my strengths? Then you start from a place of confidence and esteem and build on that base.

Take a moment right now and think about what your gifts are. Can you name five? From this positive position of thinking about what you do well, ask yourself, Is there

---

Let Go of Low Self-Esteem
1. Affirm yourself (positive, present tense, daily).
2. Practice daily acknowledgment.
3. Stop improving yourself and start developing yourself.

---

anything I could do to enhance these strengths, to maximize them, to better utilize them? That's self-development—and it builds self-esteem.

The more you like yourself, the better you will care for yourself, the more effectively you'll set healthy limits and boundaries for yourself, and the less stress you'll feel.

Hurry Sickness

The person with low self-esteem who copes with it through achievement or productivity usually suffers from "hurry sickness." Such people discover that if they are able to do one task in an hour, a sense of accomplishment and good feelings about themselves result. They quickly figure out that if they could do two things instead of one (rising expectations) in that same time period, they would feel even better about themselves. It works—for a while. Then they look for a bigger boost and try to do three things in that same amount of time. Now the threshold has been crossed. Demand exceeds capacity. It may not be possible to do three things. They start to run late, they tense their bodies in the fight-or-flight response, and they create stress instead of good feelings. In an effort to "catch up," they put their life into "fast forward"—they walk fast, talk fast, eat fast, drive fast, anything to do more in less time. As this escalates, they develop "hurry sickness."

This disease creates stress for the people around the sufferer as well. As you increase the demands on yourself, you increase your expectations of others. The raised expectations are not always reasonable and disappointments and frustrations can follow. Earlier in this chapter you learned how irrational beliefs form demands instead of preferences. See if you recognize yourself or any of your colleagues in Linda.

Linda looked at her watch. The meeting was scheduled to start in a couple of minutes, but she decided to make one more phone call. Fifteen minutes later, she slipped into the meeting as discreetly as possible. Halfway through it, she excused herself to rush back to her office to meet with one of her staff members. She apologized for eating her lunch and for answering telephone calls during the conference. When the meeting was finished, she dashed over to accounting to get some final figures for a project. In the middle of her conversation with the accounting manager, she was paged and excused herself to hurry back to her office for her next appointment. The rest of the afternoon was just as hectic. At 5:00, she ran down the stairs rather than wait for the elevator, hoping she could beat the traffic out of the garage.

How does reading about Linda make you feel? Does it leave you out of breath and feeling frazzled yourself? Do you feel as if you are reading your own biography? Linda is suffering from hurry sickness. She does everything in a rush. Her life is filled with a constant sense of urgency. Consequently she lives with a perpetual feeling of pressure and stress. She wishes she could calm down, but whenever she stops and tries to relax, she feels guilty, as if she should be doing something. Even her vacations are at this frantic pace. Last summer she went to Europe and saw seven cities in nine days.

Notice also that Linda has begun to layer activities. This means she is trying to do two or more things at the same time. While she was having the supervisory conference, she ate lunch and took phone calls. How often have you motioned someone to come into your office and talk to you while you were busy writing a memo or drafting a report? How many times have you been on the phone and started talking to someone else? Do you try to complete your paperwork while attending meetings? When you layer activities, you lose presence. You can't focus on more than one thing at a time. You'll recall from Chapter 1 that one indicator of burnout is a loss of presence. If you're doing paperwork, can you give the meeting your attention? If you're talking on the phone, can you give another person sitting in your office your attention? You're going through the motions. The paradox used throughout this book is equally true backwards: more is less. Layer your clothes, but don't layer your life!

How can you get off this treadmill? Start by becoming a better time manager. Review the sections on scheduling and goal-setting in Chapter 2. Practice saying no. Then work on raising your self-esteem. When you feel okay about yourself, you can escape this deadly cycle of pushing to do more and more in less and less time. Give yourself some times when you can slow things down. Allow yourself to take some breaks. Give yourself permission not to accomplish anything. Chapter 5 will give you some suggestions about how to build breaks into your work. Why not stop right now and take two or three slow, deep breaths?

Competitiveness

A hallmark of the Type A personality is the competitive, driven lifestyle. Behind it too lie feelings of low self-esteem. Comparisons with others push you to keep up or be better. All this serves the need to feel okay about yourself.

For many Type As, competitiveness becomes an addiction manifested as workaholism. These people put in more and more hours, sometimes with fewer and fewer results. Other areas of their life suffer in consequence and they feel guilty about this. "Quality time" has become a rationalization for Type A workaholics. Now they can justify the few minutes they spend with their families, children, and friends as quality time.

Not all people who work long hours are workaholics. Peak performers experience work as play and a source of satisfaction. However, when work feels like a compulsion—when you feel driven by it—it has become an addiction.

Competitiveness is rewarded by this culture, which puts a premium on having, consuming, and doing. We have devalued being, cooperating, and contributing. Slowly, people are beginning to see the price they pay for this lifestyle in terms of their health and relationships with others. They are asking some difficult questions: Is the next rung on the ladder worth alienating my family, missing the childhood of my children, or risking triple-bypass surgery? Is a promotion worth uprooting my family to a new town, asking my partner to leave his or her job, and abandoning friendships I've spent years cultivating? In the 1990s people are looking for ways to simplify their lives; there's wisdom in the paradox "less is more."

Bob was the manager of research and development at a software firm. After years of seven-day workweeks in which 12-hour workdays were common, he decided the price was too high. He had gained weight and was all too aware that alcohol was his only way to relax enough to fall asleep. He decided it wasn't worth it anymore and quietly stepped down. He spent the next four months traveling, reading, and reflecting on his life. He wanted to discover for himself if there could be "life outside work."

When you pursue a competitive, driven lifestyle, you make choices based less on your values than on what other people will think. You choose a career that is high paying or offers advancement instead of a career that you love. You get caught up in "doing things right" instead of "doing the right thing." All this adds up to alienation from purpose, values, and meaning and consequently from yourself.

When you let go of these external pressures and take time for solitude, you can clarify your values. You can begin to answer the questions about what gives life meaning and purpose for you. You can renew yourself.

Aggressiveness and Hostility

If you are a Type A, you tend to view life as a struggle. Consequently, you face each day, each person, and each situation as a challenge to be overcome. Just winning is not enough for you; you want to dominate. Over time you invest ever-greater energy to fight ever-smaller battles. You upset yourself over small, unimportant matters. A veneer of anger and aggression is present in most of your activities. This hostility is believed by many researchers to be a key predictor of heart attacks.

Many Type As are unaware of their ever-present hostility or are unwilling to admit it. In their minds, they are merely responding to situations. Isn't aggression appropriate when the photocopier doesn't work, when the person you want to call has a busy phone line, or when the computer doesn't do what you want it to do? Anger gets in the way of their being able to accept situations for what they are, as described in step two of the CALM model. Type Bs don't react to these minor inconveniences;

Type As overreact. They would be wise to follow the advice of Nebraska cardiologist Robert Eliot.

1. Don't sweat the small stuff.
2. It's all small stuff.
3. When you can't fight and you can't flee, flow.

Competitiveness and aggression result in a person being highly critical of everything. Such people tune in not to what is right or good in a situation, but what is wrong and what could be improved or made better. They cope with their feelings of low self-esteem by finding fault and expecting perfection. Their motto is, "We try harder."

Type A behavior can be modified. You can reduce your stress and your risk of a heart attack by letting go of these Type A characteristics. Buffer them with Type B qualities.

TYPE B BEHAVIOR

Type B people are different from Type A people in several ways. Instead of rushing all the time to do more in less time, they pace themselves and take breaks. They realize that a stretch break, a lunch break, or a vacation can result in increased productivity and better health.

Type B people also take time to enjoy the little things in life. They notice the exquisite sunrise as they drive into work in the morning. (The Type A person is pushing on the horn because someone is traveling at the speed limit in the left lane!) They stop and appreciate the extra effort a colleague put into a project, and they notice when the boss puts a new picture on her desk. Type B people do not become so focused on work that they lose sight of all the other dimensions of life.

You will hear laughter coming out of the office of a Type B person. Type As don't have time for such silliness;

Let Go of Type A Traits
                    Hurry sickness
                    Competitiveness
                    Anger and hostility
And Replace with Type B Traits
                    Take breaks
                    Enjoy little things
                    Laugh
                    Relax

---

after all, life is serious! The Type B person takes time to read the funnies in the morning paper, while the Type A person reads the headlines and the business section. Meetings aren't all business; Type B people allow themselves to enjoy the job. This ability to see the lighter side helps the Type B person maintain perspective and balance.

Type Bs have a greater appreciation for the process of life, not just the outcomes. They understand that there is an ebb and flow—a time to work and a time to relax. They are not afraid to slow down and simply *be*. They understand the paradox that relaxation brings greater productivity and they create escape hatches for themselves.

Type Bs fall victim to far fewer *shoulds* and consequently experience less anxiety and anger. They have fewer unrealistic expectations of themselves or others. Rather than carry around hostility, they ask for what they need and express their feelings. They actively use step one of the CALM model, change the situation when you can; and also step two, accept what you cannot change. Type As, on the other hand, often fail to move to step two; they persist in a belief that they can change and control every situation if only they exert enough effort. They confuse exercising control with being controlling.

Type Bs are not as likely to hold on or add on. They have learned to let go so that stress doesn't build. Rather than adapting to the stress, they are managing it.

SUMMARY

To maintain control of yourself and the stress you experience, paradoxically you will need to learn to let go rather than hold on or add on. Specifically, you need to let go of feelings, things, expectations, people, your body, and irrational beliefs. You need to set limits instead of adding on commitments. When you learn to let go, you have time to *be*, to experience solitude and restore your balance. Without this ability, your life becomes centered around doing, achieving, and accomplishing—all Type A traits. These traits are difficult to release because they have been valued in this culture. Yet you are at greater risk for a heart attack when you hurry, are competitive, and live with a veneer of hostility. Letting go gives you a healthier body and peace of mind.

Chapter Five

The M of CALM: Manage Your Lifestyle

When you notice you are under stress, you are faced with two choices. You can actively manage the stress, or you can try to cope with it. The first three steps of the CALM model have focused on how you can manage the stressor and your response to it. The last step is designed to increase your overall resistance to those inevitable stressors through healthy lifestyle choices.

Despite your best efforts to change situations, accept what you can't change, and let go of your attachments, there will still be times when you experience stress. Building positive behaviors into your lifestyle will prepare you in advance to handle those inevitable days. As you integrate more positive behaviors, you'll be increasing your capacity to respond to life's challenges.

Notice the emphasis on *positive* lifestyle behaviors. When you experience stress, do you jump immediately into some type of coping? Do you stop to ask yourself if you can change anything? Do you look at how you might be contributing to the stress through your thoughts, beliefs, or personality? Do you let go of stressors and accept what you can't change? If you're like most people, your first thought is probably to reach for something to reduce the feelings you have at the moment.

NEGATIVE COPING STRATEGIES

Unfortunately, many coping strategies result in additional stress. For example, alcohol is used widely to cope with stress. Although one drink may help you relax and unwind from the day, two is not better. Look at what happened to Janet.

It was during the installation of a new computer system that Janet first started going out after work with "the gang" for a drink. In the beginning she was the first to leave, usually after one drink. As the months progressed though and the job pressures continued, she stayed later and later. Eventually it became common for her to have three or more drinks. One night no one in the gang could stop for a drink. Janet found herself alone in the bar, wondering what had happened to her. She never thought she would be in a bar alone just to drink.

Drinking is not the only poorly chosen coping strategy. Others include eating, drugs, worry, blaming, smoking, spending binges, passivity, revenge, and aggressiveness. Each of these offers a quick fix but does not give you long-term relief from stress.

Short-Term Gain and Long-Term Pain

The problem with the preceding strategies is that they do work—for a little while. Perhaps after a particularly stressful week you feel you deserve a little reward and you take yourself shopping. When you buy something, you feel better and you console yourself that the hard week was worth it. The stress is reduced—until the following week, when you repeat the cycle. When this becomes a regular coping strategy, you have a house full of things you don't need or want, and you now may have a financial stressor in addition to your work stressors.

The process is the same with eating. Food becomes a reward or consolation for stress overload and in a short time eating becomes overeating. Soon excess weight is another stressor and a health problem.

The difference between a stress-management technique and a coping strategy is this: A coping strategy gives you short-term relief, but if you continue using that coping mechanism, over time you will have another problem. As you read about positive lifestyle behaviors, you will see the opposite effect. The longer the positive behaviors are used, the better you will feel and the more resistant you will become to stress buildup.

POSITIVE LIFESTYLE BEHAVIORS

The ultimate goal of stress management is to maintain health. Health goes beyond your physical well-being. Health also includes your emotional and spiritual well-being. Throughout the day you face challenges and stressors that demand responses. The stronger and healthier you are, the more easily you can respond to those challenges and stressors. This can be graphically shown with force-field analysis. If you look at the left side of Figure 5–1, you will see some typical stressors you might encounter. They are pushing against the positive lifestyle behaviors on the right. As long as there is a balance between these, you stay healthy. However, if the stress increases or if your positive lifestyle behaviors decrease, you can easily cross into the area of disease.

The chart can be made more complete than what is shown here if you take into consideration the relative strength of the stressors and the resistors. Look at Figure 5–2 and notice how some stressor arrows cross into the disease column. The one resistor (friends) isn't strong

FIGURE 5–1
Stress and Force-Field Analysis

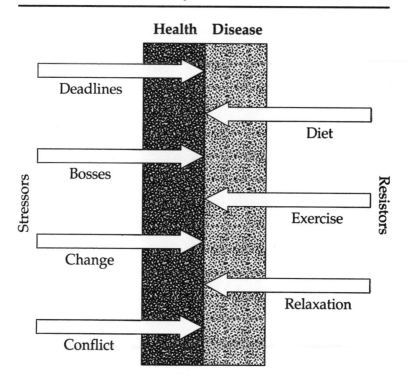

enough to make it into the health column. This chart was prepared using Janet's case as an example. You will notice that her negative coper, alcohol, is included on the stressor side of the chart. The reason is that the stronger a coper, the more it puts you off balance and leads you toward disease rather than health. It might be helpful to think of copers as wolves in sheep's clothing. If you have an occasional drink, you would put alcohol on the left side with stressors and your arrow would stay within the

FIGURE 5–2
Stress and Force-Field Analysis: Weighted

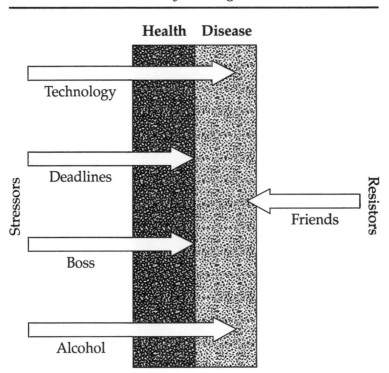

shaded column for health. If drinking has become a problem, as it has for Janet, your arrow would move into the shaded disease area.

Figure 5–3 is a blank chart on which you can record your stressors and resistors. It gives you an immediate graphic picture of what you need to do to restore balance and maintain your health.

Positive lifestyle behaviors are not quick fixes to be used when you feel stressed (for example, eating a salad

FIGURE 5–3
Stress and Force-Field Analysis: Worksheet

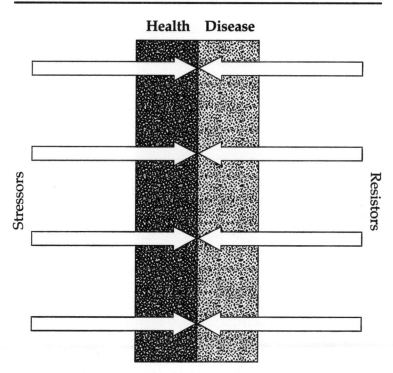

rather than a hamburger for lunch does not immediately reduce your stress). Instead, they are the results of decisions you make about how to live your life, the kinds of habits you are going to maintain, and the value you assign to your health. The more positive behaviors you integrate into your lifestyle, the greater your resistance to stress. If you choose not to incorporate these positive behaviors into your life, you are still making lifestyle choices. Whatever your choices are, they will determine whether stress is a positive or a negative force in your life. The objective of stress management is not to eliminate stress, but rather to harness it for your benefit.

Do you have to change your lifestyle? No, there are no *shoulds* here. It is your choice. Just be sure you understand that your choices about how you live your life determine its quality and length!

Now, let's look at some of the positive lifestyle choices you can make.

DIET MAKES A DIFFERENCE

Collin got a late start this morning. As he dressed, he realized there wasn't time for breakfast. When he got into the office, he poured himself a cup of black coffee. At 10:30 when his stomach started to rumble, he walked to the vending machine and got a candy bar, which he ate with his third cup of coffee. He had an important sales call at 2:00 and worked through lunch to put the final touches on his presentation. At about 1:30 he noticed he was shaking and he felt light-headed. He attributed it to nervousness and poured himself another cup of coffee to "calm his nerves."

Collin may have been nervous, but the symptoms he was experiencing were a direct result of his eating habits. Remember that food is the fuel that makes the body go. Without fuel, just like a car, the body stops running. Using poor-quality fuel is equivalent to watering down the gas. There may not be a problem with the first tankful, but if you do that for a sustained period of time, you're going to see poor performance.

Despite the variety of views on diet and nutrition, there are some accepted facts about the relationship between stress level and what you eat.

The Typical American Diet

Every country has its typical foods and traditional meals. Traditionally in the United States, breakfast consists of coffee, bacon, and eggs; lunch consists of a hamburger, fries, and soft drink; and dinner consists of meat and potatoes. Throughout the day Americans snack on doughnuts, candy bars, cookies, and chips. This diet worsens the effects of unmanaged stress and for some people it can be lethal.

What's Wrong with the Typical American Diet?

Let's start with coffee. It contains caffeine, an addictive substance that simulates the fight-or-flight response. People use caffeine as a stimulant in the morning and for the rest of the day. If you experience stress and the natural fight-or-flight response is also activated, your body is adapting to two stimulants. Then you wonder why you get the shakes and feel burned out!

Caffeine is also found in tea, chocolate, and a number of over-the-counter medications for pain relief, appetite suppression, and allergy control.

Consider reducing or eliminating caffeine from your diet. Limit coffee intake to one cup in the morning; then switch to water, fruit juice, herbal tea, or decaffeinated coffee. If you drink soft drinks, choose those without caffeine.

The second item in the American diet is meat. There is a lot of fat in red meat. "Although some government guidelines advocate a diet based on no more than 30 percent of total calories from fat, recent research points to keeping the fat of everyone older than age 2 to 25 percent of total calories—or less."[1] Most Americans consume closer to 45 percent of their calories in fat. The extra fat contributes to obesity and a high cholesterol level.

Cholesterol can clog the arteries, thereby contributing to heart attacks. The fight-or-flight response causes the heart to beat faster and pump more blood. If the arteries are clogged with cholesterol and the blood can't get through, you increase your risk of a heart attack.

Consider cutting back your consumption of red meat and eating only meat that has been trimmed of fat. Have it fewer times per week or consider using it as a side dish instead of a main course.

Egg yolks are also a major source of cholesterol. You can eat as many egg whites as you like, but try to limit your yolks to two per week. Consider eggs for breakfast a treat. Limit the traditional bacon-and-egg breakfast to once per week.

Bacon, fast-food hamburgers, fries, and many of our snack foods—especially chips—are loaded with salt. Sodium increases blood pressure and contributes to hypertension. Combine this with a high-cholesterol diet and Type A behavior and you have all the ingredients for heart disease. It's not surprising that more than half of all deaths in this country are from cardiovascular illnesses.

If you haven't done so already, take the salt shaker off the table! Do not add salt to your food without tasting it first. If you buy any processed foods, choose those labeled "low salt" or "low sodium." Get into the habit of reading the labels on the foods you buy. You may be surprised at how many foods list salt as one of the top two or three ingredients.

Most snack foods are loaded with either salt (e.g., chips, nuts, pretzels, and crackers) or sugar (e.g., doughnuts, candy bars, and cookies). Refined sugar contributes to harmful stress in three ways. First, its calories are empty. Your body does not get the fuel it needs to perform at its best. Second, sugar gives the body a false high, that short-term gain discussed earlier in this chapter, which is followed by a low. Third, sugar depletes the body of the vitamins it needs to counteract stress, especially B complex vitamins and vitamin C. These two vitamins are part of the body's natural defense strategy against stress. When sugar depletes the body of these vitamins, resistance is further lowered.

Why not choose snacks that are low in sugar and salt? Fresh fruit is an excellent alternative to junk food.

If you are reducing caffeine, fat (cholesterol), salt, and sugar, you may be wondering what you are going to eat. Try fresh fruits, fresh vegetables, and whole grains. They give you a more balanced flow of energy as your body digests them, you feel full longer, and they help carry excess cholesterol out of the body. You will find these recommendations supported by both the American Cancer Society and the American Heart Association.

Don't try to make all these changes at once. Any dramatic change is more difficult to sustain than one that is gradual. You might start by reducing your salt intake. Notice how you feel. As you find yourself feeling better, it will be easy to try another change, and another, until you are eating more healthfully.

EXERCISE: WHO NEEDS IT?

We all do! When you cope with angry customers, make difficult decisions under time pressure, manage stressed employees, and face traffic jams, you can spend the day in the fight-or-flight response. Unfortunately, you don't have the opportunity to run away from these pressures or fight anyone. Instead, you control that natural reaction and by the end of the day you feel exhausted. If you don't relieve that built-up tension physically, you will discover that even a good night's sleep leaves you fatigued.

If you can hardly wait to get to the easy chair when you get home, and if you find yourself falling asleep in front of the TV at night, your body is telling you it needs to be exercised. Exercise or some form of movement will allow the body to rid itself of the accumulated physical responses to the day's stresses.

Benefits of Exercise

One key benefit of exercise is energy. Stress wears the body out and exercise recharges it. Not only does a person experience an increase in energy, but research studies consistently show that exercise improves mood. Literally "working out" your problems makes you feel better.

Research also shows that exercise slows the aging process and promotes better health as you age. The largest expense in this country is health care. With stress implicated in 75 percent of all illnesses, it becomes imperative that every person assume personal responsibility for his or her wellness. That is the only way to reduce the nation's health-care bill. Responsibility for health is not something you can assign to someone else, trusting they will "fix" you no matter what.

Exercise tones the body. Cardiovascular fitness reduces the risk of heart attacks. The more the heart is used, the better it performs. It needs to be used regularly though. Getting no exercise is better than getting hard exercise that is only sporadic.

How to Choose an Exercise Program

Many people wonder what form of exercise is best. What is best is the exercise you will do regularly. Select something you enjoy and do it at least three times a week. This could be swimming, jogging, bicycling, walking, or aerobics. Brisk walking is preferred by more people than any other form of exercise because it is enjoyable, convenient, and least likely to produce injury. If you haven't been in an exercise program until now, it can be a good idea to check with your family physician first. He or she may want to give you a stress test before recommending a particular program.

There is a caution for Type As. Because of their driving and competitive traits, many Type As approach their exercise programs as another conquest. They set the stopwatch as they begin their daily run and upset themselves if they don't better their previous best time. If you find yourself doing this, change to a less competitive activity or stop yourself from measuring your performance.

In addition to all the other benefits listed, exercise time can be the one time during the day that you can be alone. This is especially true if you are caring for a family in addition to working full time. Honor this time for yourself as much as you honor your company's working hours.

Exercises for the Desk-Bound

Do you live with a cat? If you do, you have a stress-management teacher right in your own home. If you have spent any time around cats, you know that they (like many humans) lead sedentary lives. However, there is one thing they do that we don't. They stretch. Have you ever noticed that when a cat gets up from a nap, it stretches its back and legs? Even if the "catnap" was only 10 minutes long, the cat habitually stretches before moving on to the next activity. People who spend most of the day sitting at a desk encounter fatigue from the rigidity of their position. They need to think like cats and get in the habit of regular and frequent stretches.

There are several exercises you can do at your desk to reduce stiffness and energize your body. Among the easiest are neck rolls and shoulder shrugs. People hold a tremendous amount of tension in their shoulders and neck. If you can get in the habit of doing this every hour, you will be amazed at the difference it can make. Begin by taking a few slow, deep breaths. Then bring your shoulders straight up and try to touch them to your ear lobes. Inhale as you do this. Hold for a second or two, and then drop your shoulders, exhaling as you do. Repeat this three times. Do it right now as you're reading this book. Notice the difference?

Now drop your head gently to your chest, and lift it back up. Repeat this two more times. Now drop your head to your right shoulder. Keeping your shoulders down and relaxed, try to touch your ear to your shoulder. Repeat two more times. Then gently let your head fall backward and bring it back up. Repeat this two times. Finally, drop your head to the left and try to touch your ear to your shoulder, keeping your shoulders relaxed.

The last step is to roll your shoulders forward a couple of times and then roll them backward a couple of times. Now you're ready to go back to your work. This takes only a couple of minutes to do and gives you a release from tension that would otherwise build.

Periodically stand up and stretch. Inhale and reach your hands toward the ceiling, and then allow yourself to bend at the waist and hang limp like a rag doll as you exhale. Do this two or three times. It also helps if you can take a few minutes to walk, even if it is only to the drinking fountain.

If your legs become tired or cramped when you're sitting, lift them straight out so they are parallel with the floor. Hold them out for a few seconds and then relax them. Do this two or three times.

Millions of Americans suffer from lower back pain. This is caused by many things, including poor chair design, sloppy posture, and weak abdominal muscles. If you experience lower back pain and sit for extended periods of time, here are some tips. First be sure you are sitting straight in the chair with your lower back supported by the chair. When you lean forward to write or work on the keyboard, bend by rotating your pelvis forward; don't lean by curving your back and collapsing your chest. Under your desk keep a large phone book or small box on which to rest your feet. There is less pressure on the lower back when your knees are level with or higher than your hips. Third, you can strengthen your abdominal muscles by sitting in your chair and doing some leg lifts. Put both hands on the seat of the chair to balance yourself. Pressing down with your hands and using your abdominal muscles, lift your feet about 6 inches off the floor. Hold this for a few seconds and relax. Repeat this three or four times. This exercise can be done several times during the day like the neck and shoulder exercises.

Do you notice yourself clenching your jaw? This is the cause of tension headaches for many people. You can relax your jaw by opening your mouth as wide as you can and sticking your tongue out. (Depending on the situation, this also can be an excellent emotional release!)

Make a mental note or set a timer to remind yourself to stop and take a 2-minute stretch break every 55 to 60 minutes. It will reduce the tightness and soreness you feel at the end of the day. Better yet, why not let the ringing phone be your cue to breathe, stretch, and reenergize yourself.

RELAXATION

Exercise gives you a way to tone the body and release some of the tension that has built up during the day. Relaxation provides the body with a mechanism for preventing the buildup of tension in the first place. It is actually a process of letting go. You do not force your body to relax or push yourself to let go. Instead you allow it to happen. It's a lot like trying to remember something; the harder you try, the less you can remember. However, as soon as you stop trying to force it, it magically comes to mind. With relaxation, when you notice yourself becoming tense or uptight, you release the tension by allowing your muscles to go soft instead of bracing them. When you are relaxed, you experience a feeling of expansiveness and openness rather than a feeling of constriction and rigidity. Your muscles are supple and you are more able to flow with situations. You'll discover the truth of this paradox: soft is hard.

Diaphragmatic Breathing

The breath is the body's natural relaxer. When you exhale, you let go of the breath and as you do the body is flooded with a feeling of relaxation. You may be thinking, But that doesn't happen to me. Unfortunately, most of us no longer breathe properly and consequently do not experience relaxation as an outcome of our breathing.

To get the relaxation benefits of the breath, you need to breathe diaphragmatically. Most people are habitual chest breathers; when asked to breathe deeply they suck in their abdomen and pelvic musculature and hold it tight. In Chapter 1 we mentioned the shift from diaphragmatic to shallow (or chest) breathing as part of the fight-or-flight response. Because you experience so many little threats every day, it's not uncommon for you to begin to hold your breath and rely on tight, constricted chest breathing. That results in the physical holding is discussed in Chapter 4. Diaphragmatic breathing begins to feel awkward and strange.

To see if you are breathing diaphragmatically right now, place your left hand on your chest and your right hand on you abdomen, just below your navel. Now notice which hand moves when you breathe. If your left hand moves, you are breathing from your chest. If your right hand moves, you are breathing diaphragmatically.

The easiest position in which to relearn proper breathing is lying on your back. In this position it is difficult to breathe any way other than diaphragmatically. Don't be surprised if something your body can do so naturally and effortlessly as breathing seems difficult at first. It is like any habit: Once you have been doing something a particular way for a long time, it begins to feel normal and right, even if it is incorrect. If you want to learn from real experts, watch small children breathe: Their stomachs balloon as they inhale and collapse as they exhale. The first step in being able to relax is to breathe diaphragmatically. It forms the foundation for all of the following relaxation exercises.

Progressive Relaxation

This form of relaxation, developed by Dr. E. Jacobson in 1938, focuses on muscle tension and uses a systematic process for tightening and releasing muscles. It is an excellent way to begin your training in relaxation because you participate by doing something physical. Many other methods for inducing relaxation, some of which we will discuss on the following pages, use only your mental processes. Until you master progressive relaxation, you may find the other types more difficult.

This method is beneficial especially for people who need to use one group of muscles in their work and yet find themselves tensing many others. For example, you may sit at a terminal all day and use your hands for typing. Yet at the end of the day, your shoulders are sore and your jaw is clenched. Perhaps you write at your desk, using your hands and arms, yet you suffer from lower back pain. Progressive relaxation is a method that can help you learn to differentiate the various muscle groups and to tense only those that are actually needed for the task.

With prolonged practice you can notice when you first start to tighten your muscles. At that moment you can let go of the tension without ever allowing it to build. Most of us do not realize when we tense our muscles. Our first clue that we've been holding tension is a sensation of pain.

In progressive relaxation, you systematically tighten and then relax the large muscle groups of the body—hands, arms, head, trunk, legs, and feet. This process results in muscles that are looser and more relaxed than before you started. After moving throughout the body releasing all muscle tension, you open your eyes and are refreshed, alert, and ready to continue your day. Most people find it is helpful to have a voice guiding them through this process and use an audiocassette. You can make your own tape or buy one commercially.

To make your own tape, read the following in a slow, relaxed, calming voice into a tape recorder. You may find you can relax even easier if you have soft music playing in the background. When you see an ellipsis, pause for a few seconds before going on.

Begin by sitting comfortably in a chair that will support your back. Take a few slow, deep diaphragmatic breaths. Clear your mind of any thoughts or worries by gently letting them go. Treat thoughts like clouds on a summer day. Let them drift through your mind without giving them your attention. Keep your attention focused on my voice. Now begin by tightening the muscles in your feet and legs. Do this by pointing your toes toward the ground. Feel your muscles gradually become tighter and tighter as you hold the tension. . . . Now relax. Let go of the tension you were holding. Release your muscles and let them go limp. Notice the difference between a tense and a relaxed muscle. And again. Tighten the muscles in your feet, calves, and thighs. Hold it. . . . and let go. Let all of the tension you were holding flow down your legs into your feet and into the ground. Notice the difference between tension and relaxation. Notice also that as you let go of tension, your body begins to feel heavier.

Now tighten the muscles in your abdomen and buttocks. . . . Hold those muscles as tightly as you can. Then relax. . . . Let the tension go. Notice the difference between tension and relaxation. Feel your body sinking into the chair as it becomes more relaxed. And again. Tighten the muscles in your abdomen and buttocks. Hold . . . and let go. Let all the tightness and tension leave your body and flow into the chair underneath you. . . . Notice your breathing. Notice how slow and rhythmic it has become. If there are any thoughts in your mind, gently let them go and refocus your attention on the sound of my voice.

Now we'll move to your hands and arms. Begin by making a fist. Then bend your arm at the elbow and tighten all the muscles from your fingers up to your shoulder. Tight, tight. . . . And relax. Just let go. Feel all the tension draining down your arm and into your fingertips. Open your hands and let your fingertips point toward the earth. Feel the tension flowing out of your fingers and into the ground below. Notice again the difference between tension and relaxation. And repeat . . . tighten all the muscles in your hands and arms. Hold it . . . and let go. Release all that tension. Let it flow out of your body and into the ground below. Feel how warm and heavy your arms are as they become more and more relaxed.

Your whole body is feeling relaxed now. Notice that you've sunk comfortably into the chair. Your breathing is slow and deep. Your attention is focused on my voice. Now bring your awareness to your shoulders and the muscles across the top of your back. This is a place that many people hold tension. Lift your shoulders up and try to touch them to the bottom of your ear lobes. Then pull your shoulder blades back toward each other and see if you can touch them. Hold this for a few seconds. . . . It may feel familiar if you often tighten this area of your body. And now release. Let your shoulders fall down into a relaxed position. Feel all the tension draining off you. Gently check your posture to be sure you are letting the back of the chair support you and that you are not slumped. Feel the relaxation in your shoulders as you drop them. And once again tighten your shoulders and the muscles across the top of your back. Hold it. . . . And let go. Release all the tension you're holding. Let yourself breathe slowly and deeply. Inhale relaxation . . . exhale tension. Notice your body feeling increasingly calm and relaxed.

Last you'll release the tension in your face. Start by making a face. Squeeze your eyes tightly shut. Pull your lips back over your teeth. Tense your forehead and clench your jaw. Notice how tight each of your facial muscles feel. And then, relax. Just let the tension go. Feel the lines smoothing as you allow the tension to drain from your face. Feel your face softening as you let the tension go. Notice the difference between tension and relaxation. And again, making a face, tighten all the muscles in your face. Hold it . . . and release. Just let go. Relax all those muscles that were tight. Feel the lines smoothing out of your face as you relax. Let your jaw go. Relax all the little muscles around your eyes. Notice how smooth your forehead is without the worry lines. Notice how calm and peaceful you feel.

Continue breathing slowly and deeply. Inhale relaxation . . . exhale tension. . . . Feel your body heavy and warm as it becomes more and more relaxed. Slowly scan through your body looking for any spots that may still feel tight or tense. Repeat the tensing and relaxing of those muscles until the area feels more relaxed. Now sit quietly for another couple of minutes and just enjoy this pleasant sensation of calm, relaxed, easy breathing. (Allow one to two minutes of silence.) As you prepare to open your eyes, stretch gently and then when you are ready, open your eyes. You will feel refreshed, alert, and ready to continue your day.

Meditation

Whereas progressive relaxation is a physical process, meditation is a mental process. Its goal is to calm the mind through focused attention on a word, phrase, or mantra. One widely recognized form of meditation is transcendental meditation (TM). When the mind is quiet, the body is also stilled.

In his well-known book *The Relaxation Response,* Dr. Herbert Benson, a Harvard professor, describes the key elements necessary to induce the body into a state of deep relaxation. First you need a calm, peaceful environment where you will not be disturbed. Turn your phone off or have someone else take your calls and do not allow any interruptions. Second, you need a word or phrase you can use to focus your mind so it is not distracted by your usual thoughts. A calming phrase or a single word like *one, peace,* or *love* will work; use anything you can repeat silently to yourself that has a calming effect on you. Third, you will assume an attitude of passive concentration. This means that if any thoughts come into your mind, you gently let them go and refocus your attention on your chosen word or phrase. Finally when you meditate, you want to be in a comfortable position. Most people find it is best to sit in a chair or recliner that supports the body, including the head. If you lie down, you may fall asleep. Like progressive relaxation, this process takes about 20 minutes and is recommended at least once a day, twice if possible. As meditation is practiced, the body learns to reach deeper and deeper states of relaxation.

For many meditators, meditation is a spiritual practice. The relaxation benefits, while significant, are of lesser importance than spiritual growth and development.

Autogenic Training

This form of relaxation was developed by two European physicians, Dr. Schultz and Dr. Luther. It is a type of self-hypnosis in which the body is given suggestions to regulate some of its involuntary functions. Like the other methods, there is a paradoxical effect that if you *try*, you will not have success. With this technique you gain control when you give up control. You begin by getting into a comfortable position in a place where you will not be disturbed. Then repeat the following six instructions to yourself. You may play music behind these instructions if you prefer. Many people as they begin learning relaxation techniques find that music helps reduce their distracting thoughts. With experience in the relaxation techniques, you will probably decide you do not want any background besides silence.

1. My hands and arms are heavy and warm (five times).
2. My legs and feet are heavy and warm (five times).
3. My abdomen is warm and comfortable (five times).
4. My breathing is deep and even (five times).
5. My heartbeat is calm and regular (five times).
6. My forehead is cool (five times).

You will have more success with this technique if you have already mastered progressive relaxation. As you gain experience with this technique, you will find you can complete it with only one repetition of the instructions rather than five. This is especially helpful to people with cold hands or feet and people with irregular heartbeats.

Guided Imagery

Often, imagery of a peaceful place such as a beach, forest, or mountain will be combined with some components of progressive relaxation. After a few minutes of deep, slow breathing, and after the body is quieting down into a state of relaxation, you imagine yourself in a peaceful setting where you can feel perfectly calm and relaxed. As you follow along with the imagery, your body responds as if it were actually there (think back to Chapter 3, in which we discussed how the mind treats thoughts as reality), often facilitating a state of deep relaxation. As you practice this technique, you will discover that in a stressful situation you need only picture your peaceful place, and your body will respond immediately with the relaxation response.

Many companies now produce prerecorded relaxation tapes. You can find them in bookstores and music stores. Most combine soothing background music with progressive relaxation and guided imagery.

The Quieting Reflex

The benefit of regular practice of any of the relaxation techniques is that eventually you will be able to create that feeling with only one deep breath. Thus when you face an irate customer, a conflict with your boss, or changing priorities, you can respond with a calm, relaxed body instead of the fight-or-flight response. You'll learn to go soft instead of rigid. While relaxation can help calm you down, with practice it can become a primary preventive technique to avoid the stress reaction.

Dr. Charles Stroebel in his book *QR: The Quieting Reflex* outlines a six-second technique you can use to activate the relaxation response anywhere, anytime. After you notice that you are in a stressful situation, follow these steps:

1. *Say to yourself, "Alert mind, body calm."* For the stresses you experience in the 20th century, you do not usually need to activate the fight-or-flight response. Instead you need to activate your intellectual abilities, your communication skills, or your emotional resources. This step reminds you that you do not need to use your physical body for any of these tasks.

2. *Smile on the inside with your eyes and mouth.* This step helps reduce the tightening of the facial muscles and the jaw. By visualizing yourself as smiling, you involuntarily relax the facial muscles.

3. *Take a deep breath, hold it, and exhale.* With the exhalations, let your body go limp with relaxation. Then go back to whatever you were doing. You can engage in the activity feeling calmer, clearer, and more relaxed.

The beauty of the technique is its simplicity. Stroebel advises you to use it often throughout the day—anytime you feel tension starting to build or notice any feelings of anxiety or a change in your breathing.

Biofeedback

Another method for learning to relax and let go of muscle tension is biofeedback. Use your local yellow pages to find a certified biofeedback instructor. He or she will use a machine to monitor your hand temperature, pulse rate, muscle tension, and sweat gland activity. All these are measures of the fight-or-flight stress response. After getting a baseline reading, the biofeedback instructor will systematically teach you the process of relaxation. The machine will provide you with immediate feedback on how deeply you are relaxing. This process usually takes several weeks to learn. Biofeedback is excellent for anyone suffering from migraine headaches, tension headaches, high or low blood pressure, cardiac arrhythmias, or Raynaud's disease.

*Being in Movement*R

Paul Linden, is a specialist in body and movement awareness education and holds black belts in aikido and karate. He has developed an approach to the breath that he calls Being in MovementR. All the forms of relaxation described thus far have focused on letting go. Linden's is a model of *active* relaxation in which you are highly alert and optimally soft. The body does not waste energy or effort in constriction or tension. Instead you experience relaxed power; the body is alert and relaxed, powerful and sensitive. This is achieved not just through the breath, but through relaxed skeletal awareness. He describes part of the process as follows:

> In order to increase your awareness of how you hold these body elements [belly and pelvic musculature], consciously tighten your belly, anal sphincter muscles, and genitals, and then walk around. Notice how stiff and strained this makes your legs, hips, and lower back—your movement as a whole.
>
> Now stand and alternately tighten your belly and relax it. Let it plop out when you relax it. Next, stand and release your belly without tightening it beforehand. People generally experience a noticeable release even though they had not first tightened their bellies consciously. They realize that they had been unconsciously holding themselves tightly. For greater relaxation, allow your genital and anal muscles to relax along with your belly.
>
> As a further step, touch your belly and experiment with your breathing until you discover how to soften your belly and let your breathing drop into the pit of your belly, expanding both your belly and lower back as you inhale. This

is frequently a novel sensation since many people suck in their belly as they inhale, thereby constraining the free operation of the diaphragm and rigidifying the chest and back. When people try walking or moving in this overall state of pelvic release, they generally feel that their movement is easier, better balanced, more graceful, more coordinated, and more solidly connected to the ground.

In addition to the physical benefits, this internal physical softness creates a psychological state of relaxed alertness as well. If you examine what happens when you feel nervous or anxious, . . . you will feel the physical components of that anxiety. Feelings of fear, anger, anxiety, and confusion always involve some form of constriction and twisting in muscles, breathing, posture, and movement. However, constriction and twisting render the person unable to act freely and effectively to deal with the situation, and feeling incapable of effective action increases and perpetuates the anxiety.

If you use the physical techniques for pelvic softening when you feel anxious, . . . you will find that you are able to create and maintain a relaxed and alert mental and physical state. Whatever difficulty you face will feel much less threatening and uncomfortable, and this will enable you to deal with the situation more effectively, thereby further reducing the anxiety you feel.[2]

Being in Movement[R] is just what is says, an approach that enables you to be calm and relaxed in the midst of your regular activities—not just during 20 minutes when you practice a relaxation technique. It is one more step toward being centered and balanced in everything you do.

SUPPORT

Emotional support can be a significant protection against stress buildup. It seems to work as a buffer between stress and health. Holmes and Raye are two researchers who investigated the differences between people who did or did not get sick while under similar stressful conditions. Their research showed that the key difference was the level of social support.

There are many types of support, including material, informational, and emotional. The most important of these for managing stress is emotional support—knowing that someone cares about you and is willing to listen to how you are feeling. Emotional support implies a trust between people that makes them willing to be vulnerable with one another. You let go of the masks you may wear throughout the day and reveal who you really are—your hopes, fears, hurts, and joys. The caring from the supportive person has direct physical benefits. Students who watched a film of Mother Teresa with her outpouring of love and support were found to have stronger immune systems after the film than before. Support and love literally strengthen the body.

A helpful way to visualize this is to imagine a set of building blocks. Picture one block standing up vertically. That represents a person with a strong backbone. Now give that person wide shoulders for carrying heavy loads by placing another building block horizontally on the top of the first, so it is parallel with the ground. Now begin piling the remaining blocks (representing stressors) on top of those broad shoulders. What is going to happen? It won't take too many blocks until the structure begins to wobble and falls over. So it is with people. You can carry only so much before you start to wobble and fall over. How can you strengthen the structure so that it can carry more of those blocks? If you say, Add more vertical blocks to the base, you're right! If you put three or four blocks under the horizontal one, it will have a base strong enough to support the weight of many more blocks. The analogy applies to human beings. The more emotional support you have in your life, the more stress you can manage.

Where can you find this type of support? You can find it everywhere! There may be someone in your company who can give you emotional support, a co-worker, a mentor, or perhaps a boss. You may get it outside the company from friends, family members, or neighbors. Sometimes you can find support from others in your profession or through your professional associations. Just about anyone has the potential to be a source of emotional support for you. If you have trouble developing these relationships, you can also find support through professionals: for example, social workers, psychologists, counselors, or clergy. Today there are literally hundreds of support groups available, the most well-known being 12-step programs. There is no reason to be without emotional support for handling stress.

When you choose people to fill this vital role for you, be sure you choose people who *can* support you. A person who tells you what you should have done is not being supportive, nor is someone who interrupts you to tell you his or her sad story. A constant giver of advice is not being supportive, nor is the person who tries to "fix" your problems.

When people support you, they listen to what you say without judging you. They accept your feelings, whatever they are. They do not give advice unless asked. They tell you the truth. They are willing to be available to you when you need them. They care about you as a person and they believe in you. Do you have people like this in your life? If not, it may be time to find them. Take a moment now and jot down the names of the people in your life who give you emotional support:

My sources of emotional support: _____

_____

Be careful that you don't count on only one person to meet all your emotional needs. This is easy to do and a dangerous practice. With only one person in this role, you risk needing support when he or she is sick, out of town, or caught up in a personal crisis. Then what will you do? It's as bad as if you have no one. Try to identify two or three people who can be a source of support.

Even when you have supportive people in your life, you may sometimes hesitate to use them because you mistakenly believe that asking for help is a sign of weakness. You erroneously think that to need a listening ear is to be dependent. To want to talk to someone means you are inadequate. Of course none of these statements is true; they are all irrational beliefs (see Chapter 4). In fact, it takes strength and high self-esteem to be able to ask for help. When you make this request, you are expressing a willingness to put yourself on the line, openly share your feelings, and risk being vulnerable.

You may be surrounded by people who can and do offer you support, but you consistently turn it down. You might have difficulty accepting their support. You want to be perceived as "professional, competent, and together," never needy and never experiencing feelings of self-doubt or uncertainly. Paradoxically, this attitude projects an image of someone who is cold and inhuman, the opposite of what you really want. The strong, "together" professional recognizes the need for support and uses it. Support is part of what makes it possible to continue functioning at a high level, even during stressful times.

Emotional support can help keep things in perspective, discharge negative feelings, and boost overall coping capabilities.

LAUGHTER

Type A people have difficulty taking time out to laugh. This is too bad for them and for their organizations because laughter is healing and reduces stress. Steve

Wilson, psychologist and author of *The Art of Mixing Work and Play*, says there are three benefits to laughter. One, it reframes the situation. Two, it provides a distraction from the stressor. Three, physiologically, laughter reduces stress.

Remember the last time you had a really good laugh, the kind where your sides began to ache, tears flowed down your cheeks, and you begged the other person to stop? That kind of laughter puts your body into a profound state of relaxation, as when you throw a stone into the water and you notice ripples radiating from the point where the stone hit. Laughter starts in your diaphragm and ripples of relaxation flow out to the rest of your body. That's why you sometimes yawn after a good laugh; it's a signal that you are relaxed.

When you smile, you use fewer facial muscles than when you scowl or frown. A big smile can help release facial tension. (Recall step two of Stroebel's Quieting Reflex.) Try smiling at people when you feel under stress; you will discover you feel better, they respond to you better, and your feelings begin to be more positive.

Norman Cousins, in his well-known book *Anatomy of an Illness*, describes his personal journey from terminal illness to health, achieved through laughter. Not only does laughter buffer stress, it has healing properties. Consider how many of us have used the expression, "If I don't laugh, I'll have to cry."

Companies are beginning to recognize the positive effects of laughter and many are seeking out the services of humor consultants. These are people who look for ways the corporation can add fun to the work. When there is an atmosphere of enjoyment surrounding work, stress is lowered, people feel better, and productivity increases. For these reasons, humorists are frequently sought to speak at conventions to help establish a relaxed and fun atmosphere for learning.

There are several ways you can add humor to your workplace. One of the easiest is to bring a cartoon into the office and post it on a bulletin board. People seeing it will chuckle and before long they will bring in their own favorite cartoons. When you take the cartoons down to add a new one, don't throw the old ones away. Instead, put them into a notebook. Then you'll have them as a resource for yourself or others in your department on those days when you need a humor escape.

You also can appoint someone within the office to provide "humor breaks." Most offices have someone with a natural ability to tell funny stories or jokes. Capitalize on this person's gift. In the process, others will learn to develop their own sense of humor. Another way is to look for what's funny in a situation. As discussed in Chapter 1, you can decide how you will perceive a situation. Why not look for the humor instead of the pain? You can also create company "bloopers," which can be shared at meetings. You can create your own "Blooper Hall of Fame." If you have a company newsletter, set aside some space for humor; it will probably be the most widely read column!

Don't be surprised if some people don't get the joke. Wilson says that people fall somewhere on a humor continuum from humor-impaired to humor-powered, with 70 to 80 percent of people in the middle, or humor-accidental. The 15 percent who are humor-powered consciously, competently, and confidently use humor to manage their stress. When you see something funny, let yourself laugh!

SLEEP

One of the fastest ways to create stress for people and make them crazy is to deprive them of sleep. You can cope with whatever stresses you are experiencing more effectively if you are rested. You know how much sleep you need to feel good and be effective. Whether it is six hours or eight, protect that time. If you find yourself unable to get enough sleep, the daily use of 20 minutes for deep relaxation as described previously can compensate for some of the loss.

SUMMARY

When you experience stress, often your first reaction is to try to reduce or alleviate the tension you feel by using a short-term coper. As you have learned, copers like alcohol, eating, spending money, or smoking make you feel better for the moment, but over a longer period of time become additional stressors.

Instead of merely coping, you want to increase your resistance to stress by managing your lifestyle. Specifically, you want to eat nutritious foods that allow you to function at your personal peak. You want to keep your body strong and healthy through regular exercise. You also want to learn to short-circuit the fight-or-flight response through the regular use of relaxation techniques. When you do find yourself in stressful situations, you want to take advantage of emotional support, laugh when you can, and get enough rest.

None of these techniques will get at the cause of stress; that was covered in the previous three steps of the model. This final step is designed to build your capacity to respond to life's stressors to make you as resistant to stress as possible.

Conclusion

Congratulations! By reading this book you have taken a significant step toward managing your stress. You have increased your awareness and understanding of it. Now you know that nearly all stress—aside from environmental stressors like noise and pollution—comes from your perceptions, thoughts, personal traits, and beliefs. You do it to yourself!

Despite all the demands, pressures, and changes in your life, you can exert some control over the stress you experience. You can choose to be CALM. You can choose a lifestyle that will minimize rather than exacerbate the stressors in your life.

Remember, when you first notice yourself feeling stress, stop and remind yourself to be CALM. Ask yourself, "Is there any way I can *change the situation* to reduce the stress I am feeling? If the answer is yes, take action. You are assuming responsibility for your life and taking control of the situation with the first step. If the answer is no, then *accept what can't be changed* without adding emotional upset to your stress. Blend with reality and flow instead of resisting what is. *Let go* of irrational beliefs that upset you. *Let go* of behaviors that threaten your health. *Let go* of being controlling and remember that to gain control, relinquish control. Then invest your energy in prevention by choosing to *manage your lifestyle* for health and wellness. Managing your lifestyle will help you increase your capacity to respond to life's demands. Pay attention to what you eat, breathe, exercise regularly, take time to relax, and don't hesitate to use your support systems.

If you follow this simple prescription, you'll have stress on your side. But don't be fooled into thinking that because it's simple it's easy. Knowing *how* to be CALM is not the same as *implementing* what you know. It takes commitment and action. Managing stress is a discipline, a daily practice. More than a book of techniques, this has been a book about philosophy—philosophy of responsibility, empowerment, faith, and action. As a philosophy it recognizes the essential paradox of managing stress— less is more. You create your life, your future, every day with the choices you make, the actions you take, and the thoughts you think. This book has given you the tools to renew yourself. The rest is up to you.

ENDNOTES

Chapter 1

1. For additional information on how changes are affecting adults, see Frederic M. Hudson, *The Adult Years: Mastering the Art of Self-Renewal* (San Francisco: Jossey-Bass, 1991), pp. 7–48.
2. The four stages are adapted from Cynthia D. Scott and Dennis T. Jaffe, *Managing Personal Change* (Los Altos, Calif.: Crisp Publications, 1989), pp. 26–35.
3. Charles Dickens, *A Tale of Two Cities,* New York: Dodd, Mead & Co., 1942.
4. Gilbert Brim, *Ambition* (New York: Basic Books, 1992), p. 5.
5. Dennis T. Jaffe and Cynthia D. Scott, *Take This Job and Love It* (New York: Simon & Schuster, 1988), p. 127.
6. Mihaly Csikszentmihalyi, *Flow: The Psychology of Optimal Experience* (New York: HarperCollins, 1990), p. 49.
7. Roy Rowan, *The Intuitive Manager* (Boston: Little, Brown, 1986), p. 53.

8. Jennifer James, *Success Is the Quality of Your Journey* (New York: Newmarket Press, 1983), p. 3.

9. Barbara J. Braham, *Finding Your Purpose* (Los Altos, Calif.: Crisp Publications, 1991).

10. Hans Seyle, *The Stress of Life*, rev. ed. (New York: McGraw-Hill, 1976), p. 1.

11. Northwestern National Life, "Employee Burnout: Causes and Cures," Minneapolis, 1992, p. 12.

12. Csikszentmihalyi, *Flow*, p. 61.

13. Ibid., p. 52.

14. Joan Borysenko, *Minding the Body, Mending the Mind* (New York: Bantam, 1988), p. 3.

Chapter 2

1. Anthony Robbins, *Awaken the Giant Within* (New York: Summit Books, 1991), pp. 118–19.

2. Stephen R. Covey, *7 Habits of Highly Effective People* (New York: Simon & Schuster, 1989), pp. 185–203.

3. Peter M. Senge, *The Fifth Discipline* (New York: Doubleday, 1990), pp. 306–12.

Chapter 3

1. Thomas F. Crum, *The Magic of Conflict* (New York: Simon & Schuster, 1987), p. 26.

2. For further discussion see Deepak Chopra, *Quantum Healing* (New York: Bantam, 1990), p. 206.

3. For further information on patterns of negative self-talk, see David D. Burns, *Feeling Good* (New York: Morrow, 1980); and Matthew McKay, Martha Davis, and Patrick Flannery, *Thoughts and Feelings: The Art of Cognitive Stress Intervention* (Oakland, Calif.: New Harbinger Publications, 1981).

4. For additional techniques to interrupt a thought, see Anthony Robbins, *Awaken the Giant Within* (New York: Summit Books, 1991), pp. 133–39.

5. Melody Beattie, *Codependent No More* (HarperCollins, 1987), p. 152.
6. Bernie S. Siegel, *Love, Medicine, and Miracles* (New York: HarperCollins, 1986), p. 192.

Chapter 4

1. George Leonard, *Mastery* (New York: Penguin Books, 1991), p. 173.

Chapter 5

1. Neal Barnard, "Healthy by Choice," *Vegetarian Times*, January 1993, p. 82.
2. Paul Linden, "Developing Power and Sensitivity through Movement Awareness Training," *American Music Teacher*, October/November 1992, pp. 27–28.

BIBLIOGRAPHY

Adams, Ramona S.; Herbert A. Otto; and AuDeane S. Cowley. *Letting Go: Uncomplicating Your Life.* New York: Macmillan, 1980.

Beale, Lucy, and Rick Fields. *The Win-Win Way.* Orlando, Fla.: Harcourt Brace Jovanovich, 1987.

Beattie, Melody. *Codependent No More.* New York: Harper, 1987.

Berne, Eric. *Games People Play.* New York: Grove Press, 1964.

Borysenko, Joan. *Minding the Body, Mending the Mind.* New York: Bantam, 1988.

Braham, Barbara J. *Finding Your Purpose.* Los Altos, Calif.: Crisp Publications, 1991.

Bramson, Robert M. *Coping with Difficult People.* New York: Doubleday, 1981.

Briggs, Dorothy C. *Celebrate Your Self.* New York: Doubleday, 1971.

Brim, Gilbert. *Ambition*. New York: Basic Books, 1992.

Bristol, Claude M. *The Magic of Believing*. Englewood Cliffs, N.J.: Prentice Hall, 1976.

Burley-Allen, Madelyn. *Managing Assertively*. New York: John Wiley & Sons, 1983.

Burns, David D. *Feeling Good*. New York: Morrow, 1980.

Campbell, Joseph. *The Power of Myth*. New York: Doubleday, 1988.

Charlesworth, Edward A., and Ronald G. Nathan. *Stress Management*. New York: Ballantine Books, 1982.

Chopra, Deepak. *Quantum Healing*. New York: Bantam, 1990.

Cousins, Norman. *Anatomy of an Illness*. New York: W. W. Norton, 1979.

Covey, Stephen R. *7 Habits of Highly Effective People*. New York: Simon & Schuster, 1989.

Crum, Thomas F. *The Magic of Conflict*. New York: Simon & Schuster, 1987.

Csikszentmihalyi, Mihaly. *Flow: The Psychology of Optimal Experience*. New York: HarperCollins, 1990.

Ellis, Albert. *A New Guide to Rational Living*. Englewood Cliffs, N.J.: Prentice Hall, 1975.

Faelten, Sharon; David Diamond; and the Editors of *Prevention*. *Take Control of Your Life*. Emmaus, Penn.: Rodale Press, 1988.

Ferguson, Marilyn. *The Aquarian Conspiracy*. Los Angeles: J. P. Tarcher, 1980.

Forbes, Rosalinda. *Corporate Stress*. New York: Doubleday, 1979.

Frankl, Viktor E. *Man's Search For Meaning*. New York: Washington Square Press, 1959.

Friedman, Meyer, and Diane Ulmer. *Treating Type A Behavior—and Your Heart*. New York: Alfred A. Knopf, 1984.

Fritz, Robert. *The Path of Least Resistance*. Salem, Mass.: DMA, 1984.

Glasser, William. *Reality Therapy*. New York: HarperCollins, 1975.

Hanson, Peter G. *The Joy of Stress*. Kansas City, MO: Andrews, McMeel and Parker, 1985.

Hill, Napoleon. *Think and Grow Rich*. North Hollywood: Wilshire Book Company, 1966.

Hudson, Frederic M. *The Adult Years: Mastering the Art of Self-Renewal*. San Francisco: Jossey-Bass, 1991.

Jaffe, Dennis T., and Cynthia D. Scott. *Take This Job and Love It*. New York: Simon & Schuster, 1988.

James, Jennifer. *Success Is the Quality of Your Journey*. New York: Newmarket Press, 1983.

Jamison, Kaleel. *The Nibble Theory and the Kernel of Power*. New York: Paulist Press, 1984.

Kanter, Rosabeth M. *Change Masters*. New York: Simon & Schuster, 1983.

Kurtz, Ernest, and Katherine Ketcham. *The Spirituality of Imperfection*. New York: Bantam, 1992.

Leonard, George. *Mastery*. New York: Penguin Books, 1991.

Liebman, Shelley. *Do It at Your Desk*. New York: Tilden Press, 1982.

Linden, Paul. "Developing Power and Sensitivity through Movement Awareness Training," *American Music Teacher*, October/November 1992, pp. 26–31.

Makower, Joel. *Office Hazards*. Washington, D.C.: Tilden Press, 1981.

Maltz, Maxwell. *Psycho-Cybernetics*. New York: Simon & Schuster, 1960.

Manning, George, and Kent Curtis. *Stress without Distress*. Cincinnati: South-Western Publishing, 1988.

Matteson, Michael T., and John M. Ivancevich. *Controlling Work Stress*. San Francisco: Jossey-Bass, 1987.

McQuade, Walter, and Ann Aikman. *Stress*. Toronto: Bantam, 1974.

Mills, James W. *Coping with Stress: A Guide to Living*. New York: John Wiley & Sons, 1982.

Mitchell, Margaret. *Gone with the Wind*. New York: Macmillian, 1936.

Moskowitz, Robert. *How to Organize Your Work and Your Life.* New York: Doubleday, 1981.

Northwestern National Life, "Employee Burnout: Causes and Cures," Minneapolis, 1992.

Pelletier, Kenneth R. *Healthy People in Unhealthy Places.* New York: Delacorte Press/Seymour Lawrence, 1982.

Rowan, Roy. *The Intuitive Manager.* Boston: Little, Brown, 1986.

Schucman, Helen. *A Course in Miracles.* Tiburon, Calif.: Foundation for Inner Peace, 1975.

Sehnert, Keith W. *Stress/Unstress.* Minneapolis: Augsburg Publishing House, 1981.

Senge, Peter M. *The Fifth Discipline.* New York: Doubleday, 1990.

Shaffer, Martin. *Life after Stress.* New York: Plenum Press, 1982.

Siegel, Bernie S. *Love, Medicine, and Miracles.* New York: HarperCollins, 1986.

Stellman, Jeanne M. *Office Work Can Be Dangerous to Your Health.* New York: Pantheon Books, 1983.

Storr, Anthony. *Solitude.* New York: Macmilan, 1988.

Stroebel, Charles F. *QR: The Quieting Reflex.* New York: G. P. Putnam's Sons, 1982.

Tubesing, Nancy L., and Donald A. Tubesing. *Structured Exercises in Stress Management.* Duluth: Whole Person Press, 1984.

Yankelovich, Daniel. *New Rules.* New York: Random House, 1981.

Warshaw, Leon J. *Managing Stress.* Reading, Mass.: Addison-Wesley, 1979.

Wilson, Steve. *The Art of Mixing Work and Play.* Columbus, Ohio: Advocate Publishing Group, 1992.

Yates, Jere E. *Managing Stress.* New York: AMACOM, 1979.

Index

About the Author

Barbara Braham is a speaker, trainer, author, and practicing CALM person. She has delivered over 500 seminars across the United States to Fortune 500 companies, healthcare organizations, and nonprofit organizations. Her topics include Stress Management, Finding Your Purpose, Empowerment, and Lifelong Learning. She is the author of nine books, including *Finding Your Purpose*, and audiocassette learning programs.

Former associate director of a multimillion-dollar urban mental health center, she holds a master's degree in social work from the University of Kansas and is a licensed independent social worker.

She is a member of the National Speaker's Association and past president of Ohio Speakers forum, a chapter of NSA.

Other excellent resources available from Irwin Professional Publishing . . .

SURVIVE INFORMATION OVERLOAD

The 7 Best Ways to Manage Your Workload by Seeing the Big Picture

Kathryn Alesandrini

You'll discover how to use innovative techniques so you can manage
information efficiently, prevent paper buildup, make meetings more
effective, capture ideas, and organize thoughts for enhanced
productivity. (255 pages)
ISBN: 1-55623-721-9

401 GREAT LETTERS

Kim Komando

This book of letters transcends any previously published book of this
nature by providing fill-in-the-blank templates for over 400 real-life, real
issues letters. The disk that is available with the templates already
created is a real time-saver! (432 pages)
ISBN: 1-55623-835-5   W/5–1/4" disk
ISBN: 1-55623-833-9   book only

CUTTHROAT TEAMMATES

Achieving Effective Teamwork Among Professionals

Donald F. Heany

Discover the tools you need to fuse the talents of specialists within your
organization and get the best performance from your employees!
(250 pages)
ISBN: 1-55623-882-7

1. How did you find out about this Briefcase Book?

- [ ] Bookstore
- [ ] Advertisement
- [ ] Flyer
- [ ] Sales Rep
- [ ] Irwin Catalog
- [ ] Convention
- [ ] Other Catalog

other _____

2. Was this book provided by your organization or did you purchase this book for yourself?

- [ ] individual purchase
- [ ] organizational purchase

3. Are you using this book as a part of a training program?

- [ ] yes
- [ ] no

4. Did this book meet your expectations?

- [ ] yes
- [ ] no

(please explain) _____
_____
_____

5. What other topics would you like to see addressed in this series?

(Please list)
_____
_____

6. [ ] **Please have a sales representative call me.**

I am interested in:

- [ ] bulk purchase discounts
- [ ] custom publishing

7. [ ] **Please send me a catalog of your products.**

Name _____

Title _____

Organization _____

Address _____

City, State, Zip _____

Phone _____

BUSINESS REPLY MAIL

FIRST CLASS   PERMIT NO. 99   HOMEWOOD, IL

POSTAGE WILL BE PAID BY ADDRESSEE

IRWIN

Professional Publishing

Attn: Cindy Zigmund
1333 Burr Ridge Parkway
Burr Ridge, IL 60521-0081